I have long believed that skill in th
balancing priorities as it is the wisdc

MW01702855

that are given to us by the unexpected providences of God. *Your Life in Rhythm* offers an original and insightful approach for dealing with the multiple challenges of daily living. Bruce Miller's practical counsel for living in rhythm will yield a life that is characterized by shalom rather than by anxiety.

DR. KENNETH BOA
*president, Reflections Ministries and Trinity House Publishers*

As we are drawn into the "tyranny of the urgent" in our daily lives, we are in danger of missing out on the truly significant things in life. For many of us, life's stressors threaten to rob us of our physical, emotional, and spiritual health. Bruce Miller challenges us to consider a fresh approach that has the potential to lift our spirits and lighten our burdens. The stress-relieving principles in this book will improve the quality of our lives today and may prolong our years of productive living.

CAMRON NELSON, M.D.
*executive vice president and medical director, Cooper Clinic at Craig Ranch*

For decades, we've been chasing the mirage of work/life balance, but Bruce Miller dares to bust the myth. As both an academic who has studied the history of ideas and a pastor who deals with the messiness of real life, Miller describes a practical way to live healthier lives. His six rhythm strategies will improve your life.

DR. JIM GARLOW
*senior pastor, Skyline Church, San Diego*

Every day, I tackle a long list of duties and goals. Saying "no" is difficult for me. I want to do it all, but I can't, so I end up frustrated and full of guilt. Reading this book is changing my life. As I discover the rhythms of life, stress, guilt, and exhaustion disappear, leaving a healthier, more relaxed me, freer to serve more fully. I'm excited!

MARIETTA SCURRY JOHNSON
*St. Mark's School of Texas*

*Your Life in Rhythm* speaks to the heart of why *rhythm* is so critical for the long-term success of men and women in positions of leadership. My hope is that organizations will shift from talking about the old broken paradigm of work/life balance to the new way of rhythm, which I believe will lead to healthier lives.

TOM WILSON
*president and CEO, Leadership Network*

When I read *Your Life in Rhythm*, it was like a ton of bricks were lifted off my shoulders. Guilt disappeared and priorities realigned—almost instantly! This book gives readers a powerful blueprint for living.

GAYLA SIMMONS
*mother of two and president, Hospitality Marketing & Media*

We live in a 24/7 world that knows two speeds: *on* and *off*. But most of us have forgotten where the switch is. Bruce Miller has filled this book with great stories and practical wisdom that will give you hope for escaping the frenetic pace of modern life and action strategies to help you fully engage in the life God sends your way.

BILL PEEL
*founder, 24/Seven Project*

We can all learn from Bruce Miller's wisdom as he encourages us to do life and ministry in concert with the rhythms and seasons of life. This book couldn't be more timely for a stressed-out and overwhelmed culture.

DR. DAVID ANDERSON
*senior pastor, Bridgeway Community Church, Columbia, MD*

*Your Life in Rhythm* is a truly compelling and seminal work that provocatively challenges the illusion of trying to find "balance" in life. Bruce Miller presents a completely new time-management paradigm. *Your Life in Rhythm* is a must read for anyone desiring to "live full out without burning out."

BART SALMON
*divisional vice president, Macy's*

This book takes Stephen Covey's powerful *7 Habits of Highly Effective People* to another level. Bruce Miller calls us to a fresh paradigm—beyond time management, beyond the balanced life, beyond prioritizing our to-do lists—to harmonize with the rhythms God put there in the first place. Buy this book, practice it, and watch what God will do.

ROWLAND FORMAN
*executive director, Living Stones Leadership Ministries, New Zealand*

I first heard these truths when Bruce presented them to a group of young leaders. It was like rain in the midst of a drought. Leaders want to be fully engaged with life but not feed unhealthy lifestyles. *Your Life in Rhythm* contains both great conceptual and practical tools for readers to reimagine and restore their lives to proper rhythms.

DAVE TRAVIS
*managing director, Leadership Network*

This book is especially beneficial for those of us in cross-cultural work, an occupation in which it is very difficult to distinguish when work begins and when it ends. I'm convinced that if we understand life's rhythms and apply the rhythm strategies, we will experience a more abundant life here on earth—the way Christ intends for us to live. Bruce Miller has given me hope—and stress relief!

KATIE
*team leader, ReachGlobal, Asia*

If you are looking for balance in your life, perhaps you are looking for the wrong thing. *Your Life in Rhythm* shows you how to match your life to the rhythms and cycles of life. Here you will find strategies and road maps that will reduce your stress and give you hope.

KERBY ANDERSON
*national director, Probe Ministries*

Bruce Miller presents insights that set us free from the unrealistic demands that we have bought into. By showing us the spiritual logic of life's rhythms, he opens a door to the peace and well-being that we desperately need.

DR. JENNIE TISSING
*grants administrator, Methodist Health System*

Balance isn't just an elusive goal; it's a fruitless pursuit. It's also conspicuously absent in Scripture and in the lives of people who make a mark in life. That's why I'm so excited about Bruce Miller's concept of *rhythm*. It's true to life, to Scripture, and to the way God created us. It's a message that needs to be heard widely.

LARRY OSBORNE
*author and pastor, North Coast Church, Vista, CA*

Every now and then, an idea comes along that shakes the very foundations of what we believe to be true. Trying to live our lives "in balance" has become so much a part of us that it seems almost natural, like bars on the windows must seem to a prisoner serving a life sentence. Thankfully, this book frees us from the impossible expectations that "balance" imposes on us, and it allows us to view life and living from a better, higher, more-natural vantage point.

JIM PIKL
*attorney, father of three*

Bruce Miller has discovered a different and better way to live that allows us to fully engage in work and fully enjoy our rest in every season of our lives by forgetting about balance and by embracing the rhythms of life.

DR. ERIC SWANSON
*coauthor of* The Externally Focused Church

Finally I can throw out all those time management books that didn't work for me! And I can stop feeling guilty about it! *Your Life in Rhythm* lays out a systematic approach to living our lives in harmony with God's organic and natural rhythms.

LINDA STANLEY

*director of life stage leadership community groups, Leadership Network*

Bruce Miller brings all of his skills to bear on one of the biggest problems facing society today—the burnout that comes from the delusion of "balance." The idea that we should strive to "have it all" and somehow keep everything on an even keel is not only impossible, it's fundamentally wrongheaded. Bruce leads us back to the truth laid forth in Ecclesiastes: Life is about seasons, rhythms.

HUNTLEY PATON

*executive editor, Bizjournals*

*Your Life in Rhythm* will revolutionize the way you look at every facet of your life. You will not be the same person now after reading this book. I guarantee it.

DR. MONROE BREWER

*president, National Association of Missions Pastors*

*Your Life in Rhythm* has had a positive impact on my life in several ways. Understanding the current rhythm of my life has given me peace of mind and joy in the midst of a difficult trial.

SUSAN ALLEN

*vice president of product development for four life insurance companies*

When I was at a neighborhood playground with my kids one day, it occurred to me that there were no more teeter-totters—yet the swings remained. The teeter-totter's demise was ultimately caused by one's inability to balance the ups and downs. The swing also goes up and down, yet it does so in a rhythm that one has some control over. Work/life balance has gone the way of the teeter-totter—you can't manage it. Get on the swing; get into a rhythm. Bruce Miller will give you the push you need to get started.

DAN MATHEWS

*senior group manager, Frito-Lay Growth, Commercialization & Customization*

I find myself strongly drawn to Bruce's thinking about the rhythmic life. Standing in stark contrast to the burden of balance, *rhythm* rings true and offers freedom to truly live.

BRAD MERKLE

*software developer*

# your Life in Rhythm

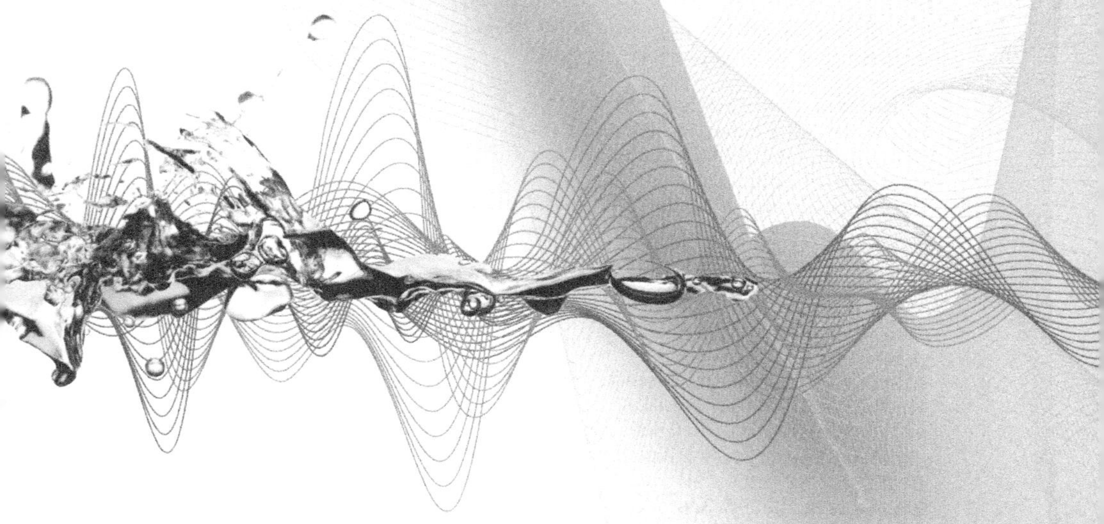

Dadlin Press
*wisdom for life*

BRUCE B. MILLER

Dadlin Press is the publishing ministry of Dadlin ministries, an organization committed to helping people develop Wisdom for Life.

For more information please go to: http://BruceBMiller.com.



ISBN-10: 1-68316-011-8
ISBN-13: 978-1-68316-011-3



*Printed in the United States of America*


**Library of Congress Cataloging-in-Publication Data**
Miller, Bruce.
Your life in rhythm / Bruce Miller.
p. cm.
Includes bibliographical references and index.
ISBN 978-1-4143-1977-3 (sc : alk. paper)
1. Time management—Religious aspects—Christianity. 2. Time. 3. Time—Religious aspects—Christianity. 4. Simplicity—Religious aspects—Christianity. I. Title.
BV4598.5.M55 2009
248.4—dc22 2009005316
Printed in the United States of America

Dadlin Press
*wisdom for life*
McKinney, TX 75070
BruceBMiller.com

# Contents

# Introduction

## THE BURDEN OF "BALANCE"

Do you ever feel overwhelmed? Do you find yourself putting in lots of extra time at work or running all over town to drop off the kids at their activities? Are you juggling responsibilities at home, work, church, and school? And does it seem you have at least one too many balls in the air?

As you've been juggling priorities and doing your best to keep everything going, has someone told you, in one way or another, that you need to get your life *in balance*? If so, you've picked up the right book.

Countless time-management systems and strategies are built on this notion of balancing your life. Perhaps you've even been to a seminar on work/life balance, which has become a hot topic in recent years.

Stephen Covey writes in *Forbes* magazine, "The challenge of work/life balance is without question one of the most significant struggles faced by modern man. I've surveyed thousands of audiences about their greatest personal and professional challenges. Life balance is always at or near the top."[1]

Jim Bird, president of WorkLifeBalance.com, says, "The demand for work/life balance solutions by employees and managers is expanding at an unprecedented rate. As a result, work-life balance is an increasingly hot topic in boardrooms and government halls today. Over the coming decade it will be one of the most important issues that executives and human resource professionals will be expected to manage."[2]

But what if this pursuit of "balance" is part of the problem rather than the solution? What if the goal of "achieving balance," however well intentioned, is an unwise, unworkable, and unattainable objective? What if chasing after "balance" only puts more impossible burdens on our backs and pushes us closer to burnout?

The concept of life balance is so cemented in our cultural vocabulary that it's hard to look beyond it to the possibility of something better. But what if you could find a way to live full-out without burning out? What if you could enjoy a refreshing new approach to living "the good life," a way to reduce your stress and increase your peace while achieving a more fulfilling life?

I'm not talking about a perfect life or a panacea that will solve all your problems. There is no magic cure that will remove all your stress and difficulties. But that doesn't mean you have to settle for burnout, busyness, and guilt. There *is* a better way. It's called getting your life in rhythm.

## Finding a More Natural Way to Live

Scientists are discovering that living rhythmically leads to healthier lives. If you think about it, it makes sense. Our entire world moves in rhythms. Seasons change. Winter gives way to spring, which heats up into summer and cools into fall, and then winter comes again. The moon waxes and wanes. The sun rises and sets. Life oscillates; it is not linear or uniform.

Our very lives are dependent on rhythms. From the beating of our hearts to the breathing of our lungs to our need for food and sleep, our bodies function according to rhythms.

If we shift our time-management and life-management paradigms from *balance* to *rhythm*, we can bring our lives into harmony with the rhythms of the natural world and resolve the unnecessary guilt we feel over trying, but failing, to keep everything in balance.

In the pages to follow, I will introduce you to six rhythm strategies. If you put them into practice, they will give you a better life—a healthier, more fulfilled life—in harmony with life's flows and cycles. Simply stated, when you live rhythmically, you will find out how to accomplish what really matters with less stress and less guilt. You will discover how to achieve freedom from aimless busyness and how to live full-out without burning out. You will learn how to relax and enjoy life more.

Your life in rhythm. This is the way you were meant to live.

## How to Get the Most from This Book

*Your Life in Rhythm* presents a new paradigm for life that has immediate, practical implications. In order to get the most benefit from reading this book, consider the following suggestions:

1. **Read the book with other people.** *Your Life in Rhythm* is designed to work well in a group or team setting. At the end of the book there are questions to stimulate conversation and personal reflection. Many people find they want to talk about the ideas and receive encouragement from others who are beginning to use the rhythm strategies.
2. **Do the exercises.** In some chapters, you will find a short exercise to apply the strategy to your life. In this way, the book becomes practical right away.
3. **Share the ideas with other people.** Start conversations about rhythm, and encourage others to adopt this life-changing paradigm.

PART I

# Rhythm

# 1
# How I Got Rhythm

*I've got rhythm; I've got music . . . who could ask for anything more?*

GEORGE AND IRA GERSHWIN

As an approach to life, "balance" never made sense to me. Intuitively, I knew something was wrong with it, but I could not put my finger on it. What alternative could there be to the goal of a balanced life?

Friends justly accuse me of being "type A times ten." I like to drive hard and fast, and I'm focused on achieving results. Inevitably, though, I get too many plates spinning, and some crash to the ground. Busyness has been a constant feature of my life. Countless times, well-meaning people have told me I need to "get my life in balance." But what does that mean?

Honestly, I tried to picture what a balanced life would look like for me, but I couldn't do it. The lack of a clear description bothered me. No one could give me a good definition of a balanced life—it was assumed to be obvious. But in my mind at least, it was one big question mark.

Were they telling me to slow down? to quit working so hard? to achieve less?

"Balance" sounded to me like something in the middle—an attempt to be average. It reminded me of when I was a kid, playing with my friend Don Mickle at Churchill Way Park. He and I enjoyed playing on the green wooden seesaw. We would get on opposite ends, and one of us would scoot toward the middle until we balanced perfectly in midair. For a moment, if we had it just right, the seesaw would hang suspended in space. But if one of us shifted, even just a little bit, the heavier end would come slamming down onto the hard asphalt.

So, is that the model for a balanced life—a seesaw? If so, there could be a lot of sore rear ends, because few people are able to keep their seesaws precisely balanced on the fulcrum.

Every time I heard about living a balanced life, I thought, *There has to be a better way to live. Isn't there a different model for a well-lived life?*

As a student of Jesus' teachings, I wondered what he had to say on the matter. After all, churchgoing people seemed especially keen on maintaining a balanced life. But in reading the Bible cover to cover, I found no instruction to balance my life. Moreover, Jesus' life does not seem to have been balanced at all. He says to take up our crosses and lose our lives. Sacrifice and balance don't blend well. If anything, Jesus encourages radical lives, not balanced ones.

In reading the Bible cover to cover, I found no instruction to balance my life.

Still, for years I felt guilty that I was not leading a balanced life. There were times when maybe for a short while I thought I might be close to achieving balance, but there were plenty of other times when I had to burn the midnight oil for extended periods, times when my life was anything but balanced.

Even though I could not buy into the ideal of a "balanced life," it seemed so universally apparent to everyone else that I thought maybe I just wasn't getting it. My stress increased because I knew I was not living the life I was "supposed" to live, and worse, I wasn't convinced that balance was a good goal in the first place.

Over the years, I've cycled through success and leadership books on how to have a more effective life. I've used the latest time-management tools: my schedule has been in Day-Timer and *7 Habits* notebooks, Palms, BlackBerrys, and Outlook software. The books have good points and the systems are helpful, but something was still missing.

## A Eureka Moment

A number of years ago, when I was speaking at a leadership conference in New Zealand, I had a eureka moment. Everyone in the room felt overly busy, overly stressed, and overly guilty about not doing everything they thought they should be doing (just like most other people I talk to). A few were close to burnout. In the middle of an open-ended question-and-answer session, someone asked about work/life balance.

As I was answering the questions and drawing concepts on the whiteboard, I had what can only be described as a sudden flash of insight: *Rhythm. Rhythm is a better model than balance.*

I'm not sure exactly how the idea was generated. We were

talking about the need for rest and for sabbaticals, but we were also talking about starting new organizations, which requires intense effort. I may have been drawing waves, giving me the idea of the ups and downs of life, when those insights somehow merged and I realized that different seasons of life call for different kinds of living. It's not that rest and intensity are to be held in balance at the *same* time but rather that they're to be in rhythm *over* time.

Different seasons of life call for different kinds of living.

The New Zealanders responded so positively to the idea of rhythm that it surprised me.

Weeks later, my friend Rowland Forman, who had hosted the New Zealand conference, told me that "rhythm" was the leaders' major takeaway. They encouraged me to put the ideas into print. Well, the ideas were not even developed at that point; they were just a flash of insight that had instantly resonated with everyone.

Back in the States, I started working with the idea of rhythm, trying to flesh it out to see if it could possibly replace balance as a fundamental metaphor for a well-ordered life. I soon found that it was a deep and rich concept that was more than adequate as a governing paradigm. The more I thought about rhythm, the more places I saw it already functioning in my life and in the world around me. It seemed so obvious that I wondered why someone hadn't hit on this before.

Balance is an inherently stagnant concept, built on preserving a certain tension between fixed objects. Rhythm, on the other hand, *moves*. It happens in time. It's active, just like our

Balance is an inherently stagnant concept, built on preserving a certain tension between fixed objects.

lives, which are not uniform or constant but are always moving and changing.

To develop the concept, I initially didn't have to look any further than my own body. I put my hand on my chest and felt my heart beating in rhythm. I listened to the natural rhythm of my breathing: inhale and exhale. I knew from science classes in my growing-up years that our bodies are filled with natural rhythms. Brain waves, for example, are not supposed to be flat. In fact, that would be a bad sign. We want oscillation: up and down.

Again, it seemed so obvious. Human bodies are rhythmic, and so is life.

## An Amazing Scientific Discovery

A few quick Internet searches uncovered a scientific field I had not been aware of: chronobiology, the study of life in time. Over the past several decades, scientists across dozens of disciplines have been discovering the power of rhythm in nature as well as in human bodies. Several major universities (including my alma mater, the University of Texas) now have chronobiology labs, and chronobiology is becoming a fairly common field of study. I was fascinated by what I read, and I began to realize that this is a deep, paradigm-shifting insight for science.

In our modern world, technological advances have obscured our intuitive harmony with nature's rhythms.

My thoughts ran to the implications for ordinary human life. In our modern world, technological advances—everything from industrialization to hybridization to the lightbulb to high-speed air travel to the Internet—have obscured our intuitive harmony with nature's rhythms.

Sunrise and sunset once bounded our daily lives. Now when it gets dark, we just turn on the lights and keep doing what we're doing. We don't have to rely on animals, with their natural rhythms and limitations, or on the natural growing seasons of plants. The kinds of foods we ate once varied by season. Now we eat grapes from California in the summer and grapes from Chile in the winter. And anything else we want can probably be ordered somewhere online, 24/7/365.

In premodern cultures, ordinary people in every part of the world followed the rhythms established by the sun and the moon in relation to the earth. In our day and age, we've lost touch with life's natural rhythms. What has happened to us?

As a pastor, I have seen personal tragedy and triumph up close. I've cheered the restoration of broken lives and cried over the destruction of once-vibrant relationships. I've watched people wasting their lives and overloading their schedules. Too many of my friends are stressed out and guilt ridden, living in self-perceived failure because they can't seem to achieve the mythic goal of a balanced life. Some have imploded into full-blown burnout. The others keep scurrying along, making the best of things.

> If everything around us functions according to natural rhythms, why don't *we* in our everyday lives?

I began to wonder: If everything around us functions according to natural rhythms, why don't *we* in our everyday lives? What if the myth of "balance" is part of the problem? What if we're aiming at the wrong target?

## Early Attempts at Living Rhythmically

At first, I began to apply my early ideas of rhythmic living to my marriage. Tamara and I looked at our patterns of relating to each other in each of nature's cycles. We asked ourselves, *What could we do on a daily and weekly basis to renew and enrich our marriage?* And then, *What about monthly, quarterly, and yearly?*

From there, we explored how similar patterns might work in parenting and in our personal spiritual devotions. The results were quite powerful, and I've since extended this exploration into my counseling and consulting with other people in various, very different, life situations. Rhythm is now working for them, too.

Along the way, I've made mistakes. With my particular personality, I tend to overanalyze and overorganize what is really a simple, profound principle. Rhythmic living is what humans were doing before they ever learned to write an alphabet or build a village. My temptation is to build a system out of it, to chart it and graph it. That can be done—in fact, I personally find it quite helpful—but the beauty of rhythm is that it is fundamental to how we are made to live. The key is to realign ourselves as rhythmic beings in a rhythmic world, not to make up and impose some artificial system.

Rhythmic living is what humans were doing before they ever learned to write an alphabet or build a village.

My wife hates charts and graphs. Even though she loves the idea of rhythm, she thought I was off my rocker trying to map out our lives. She warned me that I was going to spend my whole life planning it and never live it. Tamara and I are wired very differently. And yet we both have benefited from living rhythmically, even though our approaches to rhythm are not at all similar.

## Further Discoveries

As I continued to read about rhythm, I ran across Gail Sheehy's pioneering research into adult life stages, which she chronicled in two classic books, *Passages* (1976) and *New Passages* (1995). Though Sheehy doesn't explicitly develop the concept of rhythm, her writing about life stages opened my eyes to how we need to think rhythmically about where we are in life. For example, our lives have a certain rhythm when we're single, but that changes when we get married, have kids, launch our kids from the nest, and ultimately retire and grow old. It seems obvious, yes, but we typically ignore the rhythmic realities of our lives.

In William Doherty's groundbreaking book *The Intentional Family*, I discovered the power of rituals for preserving and enhancing harmonious rhythms in families and marriages. Because rituals are intrinsically rhythmic, they can easily be aligned with the natural rhythms that structure our world.

Because rituals are intrinsically rhythmic, they can easily be aligned with the natural rhythms that structure our world.

Elite athletes understand rhythm. They have figured out the power of interval training, which "mixes bouts of work and rest in timed intervals."[1] In *The Power of Full Engagement*, Jim Loehr and Tony Schwartz show the brilliance of *oscillation*, "the rhythmic, wavelike movement between activity and rest."[2] In their words, "Oscillation . . . represents the fundamental pulse of life."[3] Oscillation works physically, mentally, and spiritually. Loehr and Schwartz's insight helped me understand in another way how rhythm is superior to balance as the fundamental metaphor for a well-lived life. "Healthy patterns of activity and rest lie at the heart of our capacity for full engagement, maximum performance, and sustained health."[4] Full engagement comes from oscillating between high performance and personal renewal.

## Early Responses

Early on, I presented these ideas to the all-female staff of a large Mom's-Day-Out program—primarily young women with little children, some working part-time, some single, some married, some divorced, some in other relationships. They quickly agreed that excess stress, busyness, and guilt were major concerns in their lives. They also agreed that trying to achieve balance in their lives had failed to really help them. And they immediately embraced the concept of rhythm. They said it gave them freedom, releasing them from the burdensome expectations they had placed on themselves to try to live an idealistic, balanced life. Subsequently, the program director, Molly Ducote, sent me a note that said, "As a single mom, especially, I know that this book is going to make a difference. . . . Just the small speech you gave my staff changed their lives."

## Moving Forward

I'll be honest: I don't have this rhythm approach fully figured out. So far, I've experimented enough to feel its transforming power, and I've seen it work in several key areas of my own life and the life of my family. But it's still in its early stages. Perhaps you and others will develop the concept of a rhythmic life in places and dimensions I've not yet imagined. I have already seen that rhythm is a highly generative idea that touches many spheres of life.

> Stop asking, "Is my life in balance?" and start asking, "Am I in a good rhythm?"

I invite you to join me in exploring your life in rhythm. As more of us seek to live rhythmically, together we will recover what we've lost in our inane attempts to achieve balance, and we'll find new ways to live in harmony with our rhythmic world.

This is a powerful shift—one you will suspect you had in mind all along but had not yet put into words. I encourage you to stop asking, "Is my life in balance?" and start asking, "Am I in a good rhythm?"

# 2
# Our Busy Lives and the Burden of Balance

*It's the central myth of the modern workplace: With a few compromises, you can have it all. But it's all wrong, and it's making us crazy. . . . The truth is, balance is bunk. It is an unattainable pipe dream. . . . The quest for balance between work and life, as we've come to think of it, isn't just a losing proposition; it's a hurtful, destructive one.*

KEITH HAMMONDS, "BALANCE IS BUNK!"

Like most of his coworkers, Mike Jones feels guilty about being out of balance and constantly busy. He is stressed and moving toward the edges of burnout.

Last week, Mike attended his company's work/life balance seminar, where he was taught to give proportionate effort to every dimension of his life. Mike bought it. He left with a fresh determination to balance his life.

To all appearances, Mike and his wife, Julia, have it all together, living the American dream. A nice house in the suburbs, with an immaculate yard. Two cars in the garage, two kids in the family room, and two pets—a hamster and a cat. Mike has a good job with a high-tech company, and Julia volunteers at the kids' school and helps with the children's choir at church.

One Saturday morning, they pulled the Chevy minivan and the Honda Accord out of the garage. Mike took Emma to soccer practice, which he was also coaching, and Julia took Ben to his guitar lesson.

As soccer practice started, Mike's cell phone rang. He checked the caller ID. It was his boss, Gary. Mike hated to stop practice, but he knew better than to not take the call. While he was talking to Gary, another call came in. It was Julia. He let the call go to voice mail. But her second call let him know it was urgent, so he put his boss on hold—which he knew was dangerous.

Julia was on her way home from the grocery store after dropping off Ben, and she was crying. "I know you're at practice, Mike, but I was just thinking about how we haven't spent any time together in months!"

"Why now?" Mike muttered to himself, already feeling guilt tightening his stomach. "Can we talk about this when I get home?" he said, more sharply than he intended. "I've got Gary on the other line . . ."

When he switched back, his boss had hung up. Mike redialed.

"I need you in the office ASAP," Gary said when he answered the phone. "The new system we installed is not working. Needless to say, the client isn't happy."

Mike started to explain about soccer practice but then thought better of it. Apologetically, he handed the coach's whistle to his assistant, made arrangements for Emma to get a ride home, and drove away feeling guilty that he could not be there for his daughter.

There was no time for lunch, so Mike grabbed fast food on the way to the office. During the drive, his workout buddy, Bill, called to see if he was still on for basketball that afternoon.

"No, I can't make it today, Bill."

"Hey, that's two weekends in a row," Bill said. "We need you on the court with us. You said you were making a commitment to play."

"I know," Mike said, "but the boss just called. Crisis at work. I've gotta go in."

"I thought you were going to live the balanced life."

"Yeah, I'm trying. This morning I got up early and had my devotions. Then I mowed the yard before leaving with Emma for soccer practice. Julia is on my back about not having any time together, but I don't even have time for myself, let alone for her. After I get things straightened out at work, I've got to be at a board meeting tonight for the Community Food Pantry and send an e-mail to the other parents about the Boy Scout campout. I don't know if I can even stay for the whole campout because I promised my parents I would come see them. And I'm behind on my course work for the MBA. But I am on my way to a balanced life."

> Implementing one or more rhythm strategies can relieve your stress and improve your life.

"That's balance?" Bill said.

## Real-Life Stress

Mike is not alone in feeling overloaded. Maybe you see yourself in this example. Most of us struggle with busyness, competing priorities, and stress. But it doesn't have to be that way. Using Mike's story and real-life examples from my own life and the lives of several people I know, I want to show you how implementing one or more rhythm strategies can relieve your stress and improve your life.

**Jane** is an entrepreneur who publishes a monthly community magazine. She's in a difficult marriage, has three young children, and helps to care for her dying stepfather because her alcoholic mom is not reliable. The magazine is selling well, but each issue is very difficult to produce on time. Meanwhile, she worries about paying the bills, and she's afraid she'll miss an important deadline. In short, she feels stressed and pulled in several directions.

**Roger** never thought it would happen to him. After earning his Ph.D. and gaining a faculty position, he thought he was set. He had worked hard to get to where he was, and now he was making his way in academia; at the same time he was serving as a leader in his local church, and he and his wife were raising their three young children.

Roger and I have been friends for a long time but only see each other every few years. On a recent trip out of town, he started having anxiety attacks. He lost motivation for his work and felt depressed. I happened to be in Roger's town about that time and stayed overnight at his home. Around the kitchen table that night, Roger and his wife, Kathryn, shared what was happening and told me that he had an appointment the next day with a psychiatrist. They wanted to get out of this slump as fast as they could.

**Tamara and I** had our children young—and early. Our first son was born nine months and ten days after our wedding. One child followed another until we had five. At that point, I raised the white flag; that's all I could handle. (Tamara was not only fine with five but wanted more! Amazing lady!) While I worked two jobs and went to graduate school, Tamara took care of the kids almost as a single parent.

As every mother knows, you don't have to work outside the home to have an over-full and taxing schedule. Those women who juggle both home and work face an even more daunting challenge.

**Dan** works for a Fortune 500 company. He is on the success path, rising in the ranks of management. When we talked, he was being recognized as an effective manager who leads his team to get a lot accomplished but also who really takes care of them, giving them downtime after a big push. The company put him on a company-wide task force for work/life balance. I worked with Dan on a rhythm approach. He realized that rhythm could work in a corporate environment because, intuitively, he was already doing it.

**My dad** is now retired. For years, he practiced nutritional dentistry, and then he sold his practice to be free to write and speak on nutrition in his own small business. He has always been great with his hands and has fantastic small-motor skills from using dental instruments. When I was growing up, he dabbled in painting and making jewelry.

In high school and college, Dad ran track, setting some state records. After a time in the Marines as a pilot, he got out, but stayed in shape. All my life, I remember my dad jogging, snow skiing, and scuba diving. Now that he's older, his body won't let him do those demanding activities or run at his former pace. It can be depressing when your body and mind won't do what they once did.

> **Jaime** shared that his wife, **Yesinia**, is at the breaking point. Though she is a devoted wife, she announced to him one night that things cannot continue as they are. They moved from California to Texas so that Jaime could finish his degree. Proceeds from the sale of their house enabled them to pay for school, but Yesinia has to work full-time to make ends meet, and Jaime is working half-time while going to school full-time. They have two little boys, one in first grade and the other a preschooler. Jaime's parents have come to live with them to help out. Because Yesinia leaves early in the morning for her job in medical records and Jaime's classes are at night, they don't see each other very often. Jaime's job includes working on weekends, and he also needs to study, so their marriage is degenerating. What can they do?

In the following chapters, we'll see how using rhythm strategies has brought relief to each of these people.

## Balance Is a Burden

As success-driven people, we keep searching for the next system or technique to help us reach the next rung on the ladder while keeping everything together. And yet, if we are honest, we struggle, sometimes deeply.

We struggle to keep our heads above water, living in secret, self-perceived failure that creates chronic guilt. We don't take enough vacations, yet we feel as if we're not working hard enough. It seems we're always so far behind. We're not giving our spouse and our kids enough time and attention. We're not exercising as we should. We're not serving in the church and the community as we know we should. So much is left undone at work, and the deadlines are coming fast. And even though we're running as fast as we can (maybe too fast), we're still not making it happen. We're doing our best to pursue a "balanced" life, but our wheels are wobbling.

We walk a balance beam, working our hardest to make sure each priority gets just the right amount of effort and time. But when do we ever get it just right?

Ask yourself right now, *Am I balanced? Is my work balanced? Am I giving balanced attention to my fitness, my family, and my spiritual activities? Is my marriage in balance? What about recreation, friends, and volunteer service?* Let me guess what you're feeling: guilt, guilt, guilt. Am I right? I've posed this question to thousands of people, and no one has ever said, "Yes, my life is balanced." We all know that even if our lives are balanced at this particular moment, situations change so rapidly that, a minute from now, we might fall off the beam. Pursuing balance contributes to burnout and guilt.

We're doing our best to pursue a "balanced" life, but our wheels are wobbling.

Most of us want to live a full life, making a meaningful contribution and enjoying ourselves along the way. But the stress of life drives many of us to anxiety, sleep disorders, and depression. The number of prescriptions doled out each year for anti-anxiety medications, sleep aids, and antidepressants is off the charts. Life in the developed world is unhealthy. We feel as if we're wasting our lives and having no fun in the process. We want the insanity to stop.

Pervasive media create and feed excessive expectations in every area of life. People are unnecessarily stressed because they don't have a *Better Homes and Gardens* house and yard or a body like they see on the cover of *Shape*. We think that something must be wrong with us—and something *is* wrong with us.

In our attempts to have it all in perfect balance, we stay up too late and get up too early. Not having slept well for even those few hours, we're also sleep deprived.

When life is crazy, the common prescription is to re-establish balance, the supposed antidote to our insane lives. *But what if the antidote is actually a poison?*

When life is crazy, the common prescription is to re-establish balance, the supposed antidote to our insane lives.

Balance, which usually goes undefined, has become the modern paradigm of a well-lived life; its merit is largely unquestioned. Of course we should be living balanced lives. Who would want to be *un*balanced? They put you in special places for that!

I don't agree with Stephen Covey, who says that "obviously, balance is a 'true north' principle."[1] Instead, I think balance is a dead end. The idea of balance logically entails something fixed, equivalent, uniform, and average; yet none of these words describes a well-lived life. Balance is a false ideal that doesn't guide us toward health but instead diverts us into despair. It puts an impossible burden on us.

## The Pursuit of "Proper Proportions"

Balance happens when, at a moment in time, two weights on the scales are equal; it is when the exact weight balances the tire; when the stereo levels are set; when the numerical totals add up on the spreadsheet or checkbook. But life is not fixed. It is always moving. The concept of balance is flawed because it assumes that our lives will reach equilibrium at some fixed point in time. Yet, life never pauses for us to weigh its balance.

Mathematics, chemistry, and accounting all use *balance* to convey the idea of equivalence. To be balanced is to have equal values on each side of the equation. But equivalence is not a desirable state in our day-to-day lives. We would not want to give equal time to work, marriage, sleep, meals, play, and friendships. Even if the analogy is to have "proper proportions" of time for each area of life, it doesn't work, because life is too dynamic. It is constantly changing.

Ironically, the very concept (balance) that is designed to free us from the frenzy of modern life has actually subjected us to idealistic notions of a perfectly proportioned life. Balance is what one does to chemical equations and columns of numbers, not to life. People are not uniform. We are not numbers, tires, or spreadsheets. Individuals are diverse and unique. No two lives should look exactly the same—not even close. Even in our own lives, no two stages will (or should) be identical. It's not as if we could ever balance all the responsibilities of our lives at one time anyway. Responsibilities come over time, not all at once.

The concept of balance is flawed because it assumes that our lives will reach equilibrium at some fixed point in time.

Balance conveys midpoint, average. And yet, in life, we strive for excellence, not mediocrity; to be first, not in the middle. Parents encourage their children to succeed. Most aspire for their children to be over the midpoint, to be better than average. Sports fans don't yell for their teams to be *balanced*; they want them to be number one! Wildly successful people are usually not balanced. Geniuses are not balanced. To be outstanding in any endeavor requires commitment, effort, and sacrifice. Great success requires great sacrifice. Sacrifice is not balanced. And yet sacrifice is the very element necessary for greatness. Great writers, painters, engineers, missionaries, warriors, and athletes all make sacrifices to achieve at the highest levels.

## Shifting the Standard

Beginning in the next chapter, I want to help you shift your paradigm of a well-lived life from *balance* to *rhythm.* The first step is to get out from underneath the burden of balance. Some of our excessive busyness comes from trying to balance everything all at once, meaning we need to be doing *some* of everything all the time, in proper proportion. If you free yourself from the false expectations of achieving balance—and all the unnecessary burdens it places on you—that step alone will decrease your stress and relieve some of your busyness. At the very least, it will reduce your false guilt and increase your peace. Then you'll be ready to adopt rhythm as a better alternative.

> Shift your paradigm of a well-lived life from *balance* to *rhythm.*

---

LIFE EXERCISE: *Identify one or two situations in your life that you hope this book will address. Keep them in mind as you read. Later, I'll describe the Rhythm Solution Process and its six rhythm strategies, which you can use to address how to experience a better life in your specific situations.*

# 3
# Why Rhythm Offers a Better Life

*It is in rhythm that design and life meet.*

PHILIP RAWSON

My family thinks it's hilarious that I'm writing this book, because, frankly, I have no sense of rhythm. At wedding receptions, my wife refuses to get on the dance floor with me because I would embarrass her. When we clap to a song at church, I can't keep the beat. I literally watch other people clapping and try to follow them. But apart from being rhythmically challenged, my body, like yours, operates in harmony with our rhythmic world.

Life is not static, linear, or uniform. It moves, oscillates, vibrates, and pulsates. Whether we are looking at blood pressure, brain activity, or respiration, we want to see healthy, rhythmic variations. A well-lived life will find ways to harmonize with created rhythms. We're part of the great symphony of life, but in our technological society, we have drowned out the music. When sound loses rhythm, it ceases to be music and degenerates into mere noise. Recently, I was driving a friend's ski boat, and I did not know it was low on oil until a loud alarm began to sound—an annoying, monotone buzz that would not stop. That's what life without rhythm is like.

> Life is not static, linear, or uniform. It moves, oscillates, vibrates, and pulsates.

We wonder why we are stressed, anxious, and guilt-ridden. It's because we're out of step. Our lives don't feel right because we are not living in sync with our surroundings and with our natural rhythms. We've turned the music into noise—or worse yet, we've tried to manage the music by ordering its tones without regard to life's rhythms.

## The Rhythms of the World

The phases of the moon, the tides of the sea, the seasons of the earth—nature is filled with cycles and seasons. Bears hibernate and birds migrate as winter descends. Trees flower and plants bloom as spring arrives. The stars mark time as they march across the sky. Throughout recorded history, the zodiac has been used to track the orbital paths of the planets in their annual (and longer) rhythms. Days and years carry with them their own rhythms, no matter who you are or where you live. You cannot break the cycle of day and night. The sun will rise, and the sun will set.

A rhythm model recognizes and celebrates the rhythms of life. It fits our lives (or, more accurately, our lives should fit the flow of life). To get in touch with the natural order of rhythm, we must change our understanding of "the good life" by rejecting the illusory ideal of balance. It is a false god that entices us to race endlessly toward a vanishing point we will never reach.

## Rhythm Makes Intuitive Sense

Rhythm offers a more powerful and vibrant model for life. It just makes good sense. It overcomes the problems inherent in trying to balance our lives. A rhythm model honors time and movement; it celebrates variety and diversity; it highlights uniqueness and recognizes common patterns. Rhythm honors excellence and the sacrifice required for achievements while also providing time for renewal.

Rhythm is an intuitive concept that most people grasp from a few common observations. There are two main types of rhythm: *seasonal flows* and *regular cycles*. Flows are a story with a beginning, a middle, and an end—a sense of chronological development created by the arrangement of elements. Cycles are repeated sequences, such as a heartbeat or a drum cadence—movements or variations characterized by regular recurrence or alteration.

By looking at the following brief snapshots of life in rhythm, we can intuitively grasp the idea of rhythm in life's seasons and cycles. Rhythm makes so much sense that it may feel too obvious to you—like a big "duh!" That's how I felt when I had my eureka moment in New Zealand. Rhythm is so obvious, so basic, and so practical that you have to wonder why we have missed it for so long.

Rhythm honors excellence and the sacrifice required for achievements while also providing time for renewal.

### THE RHYTHM OF SPORTS SEASONS

As a lifelong resident of the Dallas area, I'm naturally a Cowboys fan. Football fans—and their families—understand the annual cycle of the game. The season is not year-round, but the cycle is. During the off-season, players practice less but use the extra time to work on strength and conditioning, get needed surgeries, and recover from the previous year. Contracts are renegotiated. Trades are made. Players are drafted. Coaches are hired and fired.

When the preseason starts in midsummer, workouts are much more intense. The coach calls for two-a-day workouts, something that's almost never done during the season. In the preseason, when games don't count, new players showcase their skills in hopes of making the regular roster.

The season has its own predictable sixteen-game flow, from the hot days of August, fighting dehydration in Dolphin Stadium in Miami, to freezing in December at Lambeau Field in Green Bay. After the season come the play-offs, when intensity increases, media attention rises, and ticket prices are outrageously high.

Athletes, coaches, and fans know the rhythm of a sport's annual calendar. Life is similar. We must know what "time" it is, if we are to live well. In the off-season, we need to rest and recover. During peak times, when the championship is on the line, we need to play through pain and push ourselves to the limit.

We must know what "time" it is, if we are to live well.

In football, it would be crazy to try to keep up "two-a-days" all year long; but in business, some type A, driven-to-succeed people attempt to maintain a year-round, two-a-day pace, and it is killing them. Burnout is inevitable, just as a football player would burn out physically if he tried to keep up two-a-day practices all year long.

We need off-seasons in our lives, too, in order to recover and be at our best during the peak times. However, to live a life that accomplishes something meaningful, we also need play-off seasons, in which we put out maximum exertion for a specific duration of time in order to achieve a significant goal. If we're trying to "balance" play-off intensity and off-season recovery, we won't do either one well.

### THE RHYTHM OF CELEBRATION AND GRIEF

Birthdays, graduations, promotions, births, and marriage proposals are times of celebration that carry special rhythms. Layoffs, divorce, illness, disability, and death are times of grief that have their own flow and rhythm. We need to grieve well as much as we need to celebrate well. Grief and celebration are not to be held in *balance*; instead, they're to be experienced in natural rhythms.

Weddings offer times of extended celebration, filled with buying rings, picking out dresses, ordering cakes, and choosing flowers, along with planning honeymoons. The final semester of school brings senior-year events: the cap and gown, the prom, the awards banquet, and the graduation ceremony. Too often, we rush through times of celebration and miss the joy of the season. In seasons of intense grief or vibrant celebration, other normal patterns need to be set aside.

> Grief and celebration are not to be held in *balance*; instead, they're to be experienced in natural rhythms.

We need to take time to celebrate and to grieve. There are times to weep and times to rejoice. Grief carries its own cycle. When we lose someone we love, we enter a cycle of grief. Grief does not have a set time frame, but it does have a common flow. We live differently in seasons of grief than in seasons of celebration.

### THE RHYTHM OF LIFE'S SEASONS

Singleness, marriage, parenting—each human season entails a unique way to live during that time. If a woman tries to live the same kind of life during pregnancy as she did before she was pregnant, she will only frustrate herself. New parents comment with surprise, "I don't know what we used to do with all our time before we had children!" What might appear balanced in one stage does not make sense in another stage.

What might appear balanced in one stage does not make sense in another stage.

Farmers have an innate grasp of seasons. They do not balance cultivating with harvesting in the same season—that would be foolish and impossible. Instead, they do what each season uniquely calls for. Some of our insane busyness in life comes from trying to cultivate, plant, fertilize, harvest, and repair the fences in every season. We are not meant to live that way. Rhythm frees us to focus on one season at a time.

### THE RHYTHM OF BUSINESS CYCLES

One of my best friends worked for the May Company, a large retailer. When he was working in the stores, we never saw him around the holidays. If you're an accountant, you experience tax season each year. If you're in the tourist industry, you feel the dramatic difference between peak season and off-season. If you're in the fitness industry, you notice that January is the time for people with New Year's exercise resolutions to show up in the gym. For public companies, the end of each quarter is intense as they try to hit their numbers to satisfy shareholders and stock analysts.

Other industries operate in rhythms that cycle every day, week, or month. Auto dealers feel the end-of-the-month pressure to meet quotas. McDonald's restaurants staff up for the lunch rush every day, but midafternoon is a dead zone. In some businesses, the holidays account for most of the year's income, and on a weekly basis, more money can be made on the weekend than the other five days combined.

These "snapshots" illustrate how rhythm is intuitive and built into the fabric of our lives. It's the way life works. Trying to maintain a uniform, constant, daily balance in any area of life, through the varying rhythms of the year, quarter, month, and week would be futile, frustrating, and unwise.

***Balance*** is a pose. ***Rhythm*** is a dance.
***Balance*** is static. ***Rhythm*** is dynamic.
***Balance*** is rigid. ***Rhythm*** is flexible.
***Balance*** suggests you can have it all now. ***Rhythm*** suggests you can have much, but over time.
***Balance*** is control. ***Rhythm*** is embrace.
***Balance*** is a seesaw. ***Rhythm*** is a swing.
***Balance*** is a rock. ***Rhythm*** is the tide.
***Balance*** is maintaining the system. ***Rhythm*** is seizing opportunities.
***Balance*** is artificial, man-made. ***Rhythm*** is natural, organic, created by God.
***Balance*** is a photograph. ***Rhythm*** is a video.

## Rhythm Is Practical

A rhythm approach is more practical than trying to maintain balance because it explicitly takes into account our current seasons and life stages. A person in the middle of career building has a different life rhythm from a retired person or a university student.

This is obvious, but actually taking your life stage into consideration is crucial to forming a practical pattern for living well.

As I write this chapter, my wife is Christmas shopping because that's what time of year it is. Most people don't try to balance their Christmas preparations throughout the year, because Christmas is in December, and the shopping season starts early enough as it is. (I still cannot fathom Christmas ads that start right after Halloween.) Rhythmic living considers what time of year it is.

Vacations should reflect a slower rhythm than the breakneck pace of getting a new product out the door under a tight deadline. A rhythm model embraces the practical dynamics of the ordinary cycles of life.

When we try to balance our lives without regard for the time of the year or month, we only frustrate ourselves. Holidays, final exams, play-offs, summer breaks, weekends, Mondays, and Fridays each carry their own distinct rhythms. Flowing with them gives us a more realistic and better life.

## Rhythms Can Be Unpredictable

Many seasons we encounter are unpredictable. Like birth and death, they happen when they happen, and we must adapt ourselves to our changing circumstances. When couples marry, the bride and groom commit themselves to some variation of the standard wedding vows:

> *. . . to have and to hold,*
> *from this day forward,*
> *for better or for worse,*
> *for richer or poorer,*
> *in sickness and in health,*

*to love and to cherish,*
*as long as we both shall live.*

But let's face it; most couples are not fully aware of what they are vowing. Instead, they're committing themselves to remain faithful through the rhythmic ups and downs of life's unpredictable seasons. As Solomon described in his famous poem in the book of Ecclesiastes, life brings times to weep and times to laugh, times to mourn and times to dance, times to gather and times to scatter, times to speak and times to remain silent. A rhythm model embraces the varying seasons of life.

## Rhythm Is Realistic

When we strive to live a balanced life without regard for seasonal shifts, we take on burdens we don't need to bear. We weigh ourselves down with false expectations that add stress to our lives.

A rhythmic approach to life offers less guilt and more peace, less stress and more fulfillment, less despair and more hope. The rest of this book reveals how living in rhythm can bring you these benefits.

Of course, the world we live in is not heaven. There is no magic system, book, or pill that will take away the difficulties of life. However, you can live a better life in rhythm than you can by vainly pursuing the mythical "balanced life."

By rejecting the pursuit of balance, you will free yourself from impossible expectations. By choosing rhythm, you will free yourself to live in harmony with the rest of life—to be content in all circumstances, to make the most of the moments, to rejoice at all times—and to set your hope on what's to come. Living your life in rhythm allows you to pace yourself, to celebrate with life-enhancing rituals, and to choose to oscillate between work and rest.

**Burden of Balance:** Guilt over not giving adequate attention to every priority every time

***Benefit of Rhythm:*** Peace in releasing expectations that do not fit this time in life and in setting a healthy pace for activities

**Burden of Balance:** Busyness in trying to care for every responsibility in every season and stage

***Benefit of Rhythm:*** Fulfillment in seizing the unique opportunities offered by each season and in building life-enhancing rituals

**Burden of Balance:** Stress in the attempt to keep everything proportionate at all times

***Benefit of Rhythm:*** Joy in embracing the blessings of each time and the oscillation of work and rest

**Burden of Balance:** Despair over being stuck in the impossible pursuit of keeping everything in balance

***Benefit of Rhythm:*** Hope in anticipating a new season ahead and the ultimate rhythm that is sure to come

## Rhythm Is Not an Excuse for Inaction

Amy, an elementary-age girl, heard me talk on the topic of rhythmic living. On the way home, she said to her mother, "Someone could use rhythm as an excuse not to do stuff." (Out of the mouths of babes . . . )

Obviously, it would be easy for a person to abuse this concept: "I can't take on that project because it doesn't fit my life's rhythm." "I'm ignoring my family right now because I am in a getting-the-business-ramped-up rhythm." And so on.

The antidote to misapplied rhythm is intentional living. This book assumes you have a life mission that guides you. A life mission provides the boundaries within which your life's rhythms can oscillate and flow. If you haven't yet established a life mission, you don't have the direction you need to guide your rhythms. Having a life mission is an important first step toward getting your life into rhythm.

> Having a life mission is an important first step toward getting your life into rhythm.

This book also assumes that you are taking responsibility for the stewardships you have been granted. For example, if you have children, you are responsible to be a good father or mother. If you have a job, you are responsible to do it well. As a member of the human race, living in community on this planet, you have basic responsibilities. As a created being, you have responsibilities to God. Living rhythmically will help you carry out your stewardship responsibilities to the One to whom you will give account one day. It is your life's mission and your stewardships that guide you and prevent you from abusing the concept of rhythm.

## Is *Rhythm* vs. *Balance* Just a Word Game?

Is there really a difference in everyday life between balance and rhythm? Are we not still juggling the same number of balls, but just thinking about them differently? Frankly, some of the practical advice that has been attached to the balance model makes great sense. Of course you should eat well, get good rest, and exercise regularly. Of course you should not work yourself to death or slump in the easy chair all night watching TV. But most of the good practical advice offered in the name of balance fits better in the paradigm of rhythm.

And yet a rhythm approach offers more than just the same old practical advice in a new frame. It is a fresh model that enables you to look differently at how you live. There are six rhythm strategies that give you a way to live a better life.

Let's look now at the two kinds of rhythm that undergird the six rhythm strategies.

# 4
# Kairos and Chronos Rhythms

*Time is nature's way of preventing everything from happening all at once.*

MARK TWAIN

The concept of time seems simple until we start trying to understand what it really means. In some ways, time is linear and regular and moves at a consistent pace—minute by minute, hour by hour, day by day, and so on. Our experience of time, however, can vary greatly, depending on what we're doing. We talk about how time flies when we're having fun or how a day can drag on forever if we're doing something we don't enjoy. So time is linear and consistent, but it also seems to flow and vary.

When I got home from New Zealand and began to develop the idea of using rhythm rather than balance as a means of understanding and managing time, I started taking note of all the natural rhythms of life that I could observe. I soon discovered that rhythms come in two basic types—recurring and nonrecurring. Some rhythms, such as heartbeats or sunrises, recur repeatedly in a fairly regular pattern. Other rhythms have patterns but not recurrence. For instance, our lives follow a pattern from birth to childhood to adolescence to young adulthood to middle age, and so on, but we experience each phase of life only once. Our lives are a seasonal flow. We experience fairly predictable stages, but they are unidirectional (linear).

Music can carry both cyclical and linear rhythms, especially in a longer piece such as an opera or symphony. Most music has rhythm, and songs have meter. But a symphony has movement as well as meter; there is a beginning, a middle, and an end.

The ocean has a patterned but unpredictable, noncyclical rhythm to it. Sometimes the water is calm; at other times a storm crashes waves onto the coastline. Even with all our modern technology, we still cannot fully predict the weather or the rhythm of the ocean. We are still surprised by sudden waves such as a tsunami.

In a different way, the sky has a rhythm to it. The planets and stars move in largely cyclical, predictable patterns. We can look to the sky to know what time of day it is. The moon tells us what time of the month it is. The lengths of days and nights, tied to the tilt of the earth in relation to the sun, tell us what season it is. The stars can tell us the time of year. These are cyclical, predictable patterns. The day/night cycle is one of the most basic natural cycles. This circadian rhythm structures our earthly lives. We experience life in nature's cycles, determined by the sky—the relative movements of the sun, moon, and earth.

In our lives, we see both types of rhythm emerge: a flow, such as is created in a story or as our lives move from day to day and from year to year, and a regular recurrence, in uniform patterns, such as our daily, weekly, and monthly schedules. We live in both cyclical patterns and seasonal flows.

> In our lives, we see both types of rhythm. . . . We live in both cyclical patterns and seasonal flows.

Life is full of unique seasons, from engagement to pregnancy to grief. Some of these we experience more than once, but never in the same way. No two times of grief are identical. Seasons are like the waves of the sea; some you see coming, and some you don't. Each wave has a pattern to it, but no two waves are exactly alike.

## Two Kinds of Time

My son Jimmy has always been fascinated by mythology—so much so that he even studied it in college. When he heard that I was exploring the concept of time in terms of rhythm, he let me know that the ancient Greeks had already beaten me to it.

It turns out that in Greek mythology, there are two gods associated with the two different kinds of time, which roughly correspond to the Greek words *chronos* and *kairos*.

*Chronos* corresponds to regular cycles, and *kairos* corresponds to progressive flows.[1] Chronos is *clock and calendar time*, measurable and predictable, recurring in known cycles. Kairos is *experienced time*, which is nonrecurring and not as predictable, but it flows. Kairos is *quality time*, such as when we talk about having a good time together, finding the right time to say something sensitive, or looking for the right time to make an investment.

In some Greco-Roman mosaics, the god Chronos is depicted as a man turning a zodiac. In early works, he is the personification of time emerging from primordial chaos. In more modern times, he has become Father Time, the old, wise-looking man with a long gray beard whose curved scythe was originally a curve of the zodiac circle. The god Kairos was the youngest son of Zeus. He is believed to be the spirit of opportunity. Aesop, in his fables, describes Kairos as running swiftly; he is bald except for a lock of hair on his forehead, which must be grabbed from the front. Kairos can be grasped only as he approaches. Once he has passed you, not even Zeus can pull him back. Opportunity is that brief moment in which things are possible.

Lexically, *chronos* relates to motion. It is a physical concept and thus quantifiable.[2] Its origin is associated with the movement of celestial bodies. Typically, *chronos* denotes time in general or a section of time, such as a part of a year. Plato and Aristotle linked *chronos* with movement and change. In the New Testament, *chronos* often refers to a span of time, but it can also be used to designate a special season.[3]

In contrast, the earliest linguistic sense of the word *kairos* is the "decisive or crucial place or point." In the adage "Know the time" (*kairon gnothi*), *kairos* means "Know the critical situation in your life, know that it demands a decision, and what decision, train yourself to recognize as such the decisive point in your life, and to act accordingly."[4] *Kairos* refers to the decisive moment when you can seize the opportunity in front of you. It can be dangerous or propitious. It carries with it a sense that destiny demands timely action.

In the Septuagint, the Greek version of the Old Testament, *kairos* shifts to a sense of divine appointment or a time of judgment. It can mean the "right moment," a propitious hour.

Though it is sometimes used in a purely temporal sense in the New Testament, *kairos* is mainly used for specific and decisive points in history and in an individual's life.[5]

## Two Kinds of Rhythm Strategies

For the purposes of this book, I am using the concepts of *chronos* and *kairos* to label the two basic kinds of rhythm: cycles and seasons. We live rhythmically by following the sky's patterns, which form our chronos rhythms (cycles), and by riding the sea waves of our kairos rhythms (seasons).

> *Kairos* refers to the decisive moment when you can seize the opportunity in front of you.

We all live in the same world, structured by five fundamental chronos cycles: solar, seasonal, lunar, sabbatical, and rotational; in other words, the year, quarter, month, week, and day. We also live in kairos seasons: unique times such as the birth of a child, the college years, rehabilitation after an injury, retirement, or moving to a new city. We ride the waves of life as they come. Chronos cycles describe the temporal context of our environment on planet Earth, whereas kairos seasons describe patterns in the flow of our human lives.

Kairos seasons are not tied to clock time. They are flows rather than cycles, the movement of a story rather than the meter of a tune. Kairos is an opportune time, the right time to say or do something. When a man decides to propose marriage, he looks for the "right time," which has little to do with a clock or a calendar. It has to do with emotions and a sense of appropriateness.

The chronos cycles describe cyclical, recurring rhythms built into the fabric of the created order, environmental rhythms established by astronomical phenomena and embedded in our biology. In contrast, kairos seasons are linear, noncyclical, human rhythms.

Many individual kairos seasons have a predictable flow. Adolescence brings common struggles and triumphs. A season of grief carries a cycle that people experience in a typical pattern. Most of us will experience several major grief cycles in our lifetimes, along with many smaller ones. However, a grief cycle is very different from a lunar/monthly cycle. Grief does not happen for everyone at the same time. It is not based on astronomical movements. It is linear, not cyclical.

Chronos cycles are known and constant. We can be sure that summer is coming. Year will follow after year, month after month. In contrast, kairos seasons are often unpredictable. Some can be anticipated, but many are total surprises. We know we are going to get older, but we do not know what tomorrow might hold. Life events such as finding a spouse, losing a job, inheriting a fortune, or losing physical capacity are all examples of unpredictable kairos seasons.

Chronos is about measured time. Kairos is about experienced time. Chronos is chronological time, counted on clocks and calendars. A kairos season is experienced as a good time and a bad time or the right time and the wrong time. When you are on a three-hour date with the one you love, time flies. When you are in a boring, three-hour lecture, time crawls. The chronos time is the same: three hours. The kairos time is very different: flying versus crawling.

Chronos cycles are known and constant. . . . Chronos is about measured time.

While chronos involves the *quantity* of time an activity takes, kairos looks at the *quality* of that time. Chronos is limited to regular measurements. Kairos considers events, such as the

Chronos Cycles: measured time
*Kairos Seasons:* experienced time
Chronos Cycles: quantity of time
*Kairos Seasons:* quality of time
Chronos Cycles: clock or calendar time
*Kairos Seasons:* heart time
Chronos Cycles: cyclical
*Kairos Seasons:* linear
Chronos Cycles: recurrence
*Kairos Seasons:* occurrence
Chronos Cycles: predictable pattern
*Kairos Seasons:* unpredictable pattern
Chronos Cycles: uniform
*Kairos Seasons:* unique
Chronos Cycles: oscillating
*Kairos Seasons:* progressing
Chronos Cycles: heartbeat
*Kairos Seasons:* lifetime
Chronos Cycles: a song's meter
*Kairos Seasons:* a symphony's movement
Chronos Cycles: ritual
*Kairos Seasons:* hope
Chronos Cycles: pace
*Kairos Seasons:* opportunity
Chronos Cycles: tradition
*Kairos Seasons:* anticipation
Chronos Cycles: chronological
*Kairos Seasons:* phenomenological

time a king reigned, the digital age, the time when communism collapsed in Russia, or the time you fell in love at the beach. These times are not hours, days, weeks, or even years; they are descriptions of something that happened. When we pray for a time when peace will cover the earth, we are not talking about a date but a quality of life.

On a more personal scale, we speak of kairos seasons when we use the word *time* to describe periods in our own lives. "Remember when we were best friends?" "Remember the time we had that fluffy dog?" "Remember when Dad was working at home?" "Remember when we lived in the apartment?" These are not merely descriptions of dates or quantities of chronos time; they are also descriptions of lived experiences, a quality of that time, the way it felt.

A kairos moment can be as simple as the right time to say something sensitive to your friend. Proverbs 15:23 says, "A man finds joy in giving an apt reply—and how good is a timely word!" This kind of "right time" cannot be set on a clock but must be discerned by the heart.

Paying attention to kairos seasons can add tremendous value to our lives. These rhythms are even more powerful than chronos cycles. Even though kairos seasons are more difficult to discern, they are more important to grasp. Kairos moments can be seized as opportunities, enjoyed for their blessing, or resented for their difficulties. In any given season, we want to release expectations that don't fit that time as well as anticipate what comes next.

PART II

# Kairos Rhythm Strategies

# 5
# Your Personal Seasons and Life Stages

*What holds music together? Rhythm. What holds our lives together? Rhythm. Is your world a world without music? Is your life a song without rhythm? . . . In this day and age—in a world obsessed with speed, noise, greed, lust, and activity—the rhythm of life is a radical, countercultural, revolutionary act.*

MATTHEW KELLY, *THE RHYTHM OF LIFE*

One October, off the coast near Santa Monica, California, Tamara and I watched a surfing competition. As a series of waves formed on the horizon, the surfers could gauge pretty accurately which ones would result in a ride worth taking and which would be duds to let pass by.

When the surfers decided to take a wave, they obviously had a plan. I saw them paddle hard up onto the wave and stand up on their boards just as it crested. As the wave carried them toward the shore, the surfers would work the wave, moving slightly up and down the face to keep riding the wave as long as they could.

You can't ride the waves if you don't see them or if you misjudge them. Surfers learn how to read the waves and how to take advantage of the natural swells and breaks. In this chapter, we will look at how to identify the waves of kairos rhythms in our personal seasons and life stages. Then in the following three chapters, we will explore three kairos rhythm strategies that will enable us to ride the waves well.

## Solomon's Wisdom

Though we find no instruction about *balance* in the Bible, there is a famous poem crafted by King Solomon, the wisest man who ever lived, that portrays a rhythmic approach to life—Ecclesiastes 3:1-8. In the late 1950s, folksinger Pete Seeger turned it into the song "Turn, Turn, Turn," which was later recorded by a number of bands in the 1960s, including the most famous, The Byrds.

In fourteen couplets, each a pair of opposites, Solomon covers a wide range of human activity. Twenty-eight times, the word *time* is repeated as King Solomon makes the point that God gives us rhythms in which we are to live.

> *There is a time for everything, and a season for every activity under heaven:*
> *a time to be born and a time to die,*
> *a time to plant and a time to uproot,*
> *a time to kill and a time to heal,*
> *a time to tear down and a time to build,*
> *a time to weep and a time to laugh,*
> *a time to mourn and a time to dance,*
> *a time to scatter stones and a time to gather them,*
> *a time to embrace and a time to refrain,*
> *a time to search and a time to give up,*

*a time to keep and a time to throw away,*
*a time to tear and a time to mend,*
*a time to be silent and a time to speak,*
*a time to love and a time to hate,*
*a time for war and a time for peace.*

Although it is common to hear Solomon's poem used to validate the paradigm of balance, it actually doesn't. Solomon is not saying to hold all activities in balance, but to realize that different seasons call for different activities, different rhythms. For instance, when he writes, "There is . . . a time to be silent and a time to speak," he's not suggesting that we try to balance speaking and silence. Rather, Solomon is saying there are times to speak up and times to be silent—each in its own season and rhythm.

Solomon uses a Hebrew word for "time" that refers to more than chronological time; it suggests an occasion or a season of time—what in Greek would be a kairos moment. Rather than seeking an artificial balance, Solomon is challenging us to live full-out in each and every season. When it is time to love, love with all your heart; when it is time to hate injustice, hate it passionately. When it is time to mourn, mourn fully. When it is time to dance, dance with everything you've got. Live full-out.

The poem encompasses the most momentous events of human life—its beginning and end, its times of creative and destructive activities, its private and public emotions. These are not times we choose but ones we accept. Kairos seasons. In the *Anchor Bible Commentary*, Choon-Leong Seow writes, "Indeed, people do not decide when to heal, weep, laugh, mourn, lose, love, hate, or be in war or peace. These are occasions in which people find themselves, and they can only respond to them. All that mortals can do in the face of these times is to be open to them."[1]

There is no balance to be struck between birth and death, planting and uprooting, weeping and laughing. Instead, when we live our lives in rhythm, we're free to give ourselves fully to every kairos season. We are not to be born and die, plant and uproot, weep and laugh *in balance at the same time*, but *in rhythm at different times*. Further, Solomon's point is not for us to manage our lives so that we balance activities in any one season; instead, we're to flow with life through differing seasons, each carrying its own unique emotions and activities. These kinds of human rhythms are part and parcel of kairos seasons.

When we live our lives in rhythm, we're free to give ourselves fully to every kairos season.

Each aspect of life has its time and season; thus, we need to *understand the times* (see 1 Chronicles 12:32). Living well involves having the wisdom to know the times and having the faith in God to accept that our times are in his hands (see Psalm 31:15). From God's point of view, in light of eternity, all times are "beautiful" or "appropriate" (see Ecclesiastes 3:11).[2]

Solomon's point is that meaning in life can be found by seeking to "fear" (honor and obey) God and to enjoy life. We are to accept what God has given and rejoice in his gifts. With such an approach, we can replace despair and frustration with contentment.[3] If we live in harmony with God's rhythms, we can discover more peace, fulfillment, joy, and hope. It is not so much that there is a *correct* time to do everything as it is that if we are living in rhythm with God's timing, life will not be meaningless. Everything will be beautiful or appropriate in its time, even difficult experiences.[4]

King Solomon, a man who lived life to the full, concluded

that we cannot explain life but must experience it. We can either endure it or enjoy it. Embracing kairos rhythms enables us to live full-out while at the same time enjoying a deep inner peace—a peace that comes from being in harmony with God's rhythms.

## Two Kinds of Kairos Rhythms

Kairos rhythms are most easily understood in relation to *personal seasons* and *life stages*. These seasons and stages are more linear than cyclical. We move through them rather than repeating them. Some seasons we may experience more than once, but never in exactly the same way. Personal seasons typically last from a month to five years. These include events such as pregnancy, grief, play-offs, building a home, moving to a new city, and job changes.

Kairos rhythms are most easily understood in relation to *personal seasons* and *life stages*.

Life stages are longer periods such as adolescence, midlife, and retirement, which typically last from four to twenty-five years. Sometimes seasons overlap or coincide with stages, such as when we go to college during our late adolescent to early adult stage. It isn't as important to *categorize* our seasons and stages as it is to *understand* what time it is in our lives and to live in sync with the rhythm of that time.

## PERSONAL SEASONS

> *There is a time for everything, . . . a time to weep and a time to laugh.*
>
> ECCLESIASTES 3:1, 4

Personal seasons are not so much based on chronological age as they are identified by *significant experiences.* A season is a period of time characterized by unique features that set it apart from other times in our lives. For instance, pregnancy is a nine-month season that is quite distinct from all other seasons in life. And mothers will experience the season of pregnancy in different ways than fathers will. This kind of distinction can be true of other common seasons as well.

> We must make the necessary adjustments in our lives to release inappropriate expectations, seize opportunities, and anticipate what's next.

The start of a season is not always predictable, but once it starts, its cycle usually follows a common pattern. Still, it is difficult to classify personal seasons because they are so diverse and numerous. Are you starting a new job? moving to a new home? going back to school? Are you rehabilitating after an injury or recovering from an accident? Have you buried a close friend? Are you engaged to be married? There are thousands of common seasons. Some seasons are restful; others are taxing and tiring.

When a personal season begins, we first must recognize it for what it is, then make the necessary adjustments in our lives to release inappropriate expectations, seize opportunities, and anticipate what's next.

### *Grief*

When a loved one dies, it feels as if the whole world should stop. That feeling is a signal to stop the current flow of our lives to take time to grieve. The cycle of grief takes time, energy, and work to get through. We need to give ourselves to grieving well.

But it's not just death that sets into motion a cycle of grief. Any major loss brings grief: divorce, being fired from a job, losing a substantial part of your retirement savings in a stock-market downturn, having your home foreclosed. When physical capabilities are taken away by accident or illness, we grieve. When we lose a good friend, we grieve. When our best-laid plans turn to dust, we grieve.

A typical pattern of grief was first articulated by Swiss-born psychiatrist Elisabeth Kübler-Ross, whose book *On Death and Dying* became a foundational text in the study of grief.[5]

Most psychologists and counselors today accept Kübler-Ross's model of five basic stages of grief: denial, anger, bargaining, depression, and acceptance. These stages can occur in a different order and in varying degrees of intensity. But when we are in a season of grief, we cannot live well if we attempt to ignore the grief cycle.

Not every personal season is as well understood as the grief cycle, but as with grief, if we try to avoid a natural rhythm, or if we fight against it, we create physical and emotional health problems.

## The Grief Cycle[6]

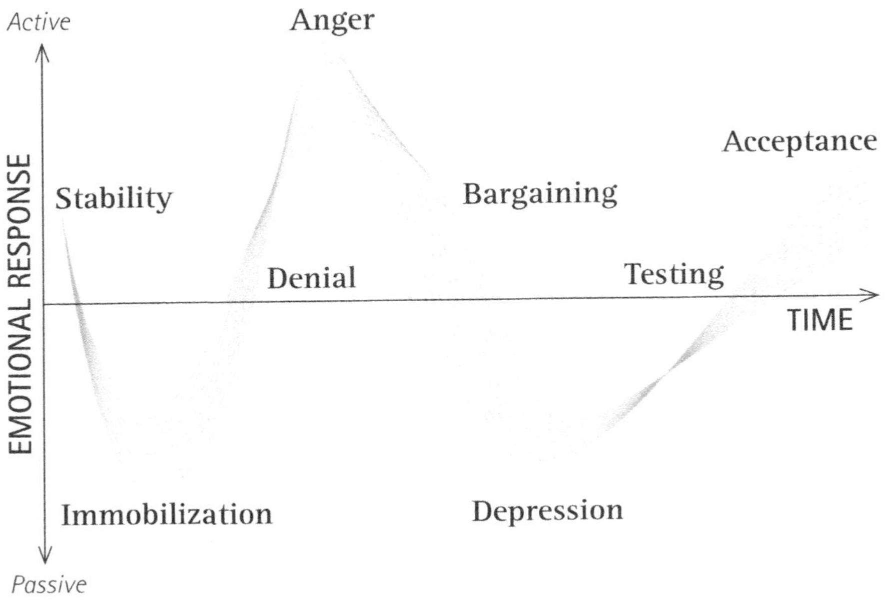


*Beginnings and endings*

Many seasons are characterized by a beginning or an ending. Often, when one season ends, another begins. Conception begins the season of pregnancy, the beginning of new life. The birth of a baby concludes pregnancy and launches both a season of newborn care and an entire stage of parenting. A new relationship with a friend creates a season of learning and discovery as you gradually share your story and yourself with the other person. Starting a business introduces a season of intense activity. Moving to a new city begins a season of starting over that lasts about a year. If you decide to remodel part of your home, you set in motion a season of physical labor and disruption of your normal routine.

Relational beginnings—such as with a new boyfriend or girlfriend, spouse, or child—have a major effect on our lives. On a much different level, a new boss, employee, client, or tennis partner creates a smaller, but still new, relational rhythm.

Endings often constitute seasons as well. When a significant relationship ends, we grieve. The intimacy and length of the relationship affect the extent of our grief. The loss of a pet, a friend, or a home—or more internal losses, such as the loss of faith or security—entails a season of recovery.

### *Recovery*

Recovery itself is a class of seasons. When we suffer an illness or injury, we require a season of recovery and rehabilitation. In sports, the off-season provides a time of recovery from the rigors of the season. In school, summer vacation offers refreshment from the demands of study. Sabbaticals are seasons of renewal that some professors and pastors enjoy.

### *Crisis*

Crises bring a rhythm similar to the grief cycle. A back injury from a car accident or an illness leading to extended hospitalization is a crisis that will require a time of recovery. A house fire, a criminal break-in or theft, or a sudden drop in the stock market can generate a time of increased fear and insecurity. Depending on the extent of the damage, a fire can result in a time of rebuilding, dealing with insurance companies, even relocating. All trauma requires a time of recovery, which might be physical, emotional, spiritual, and/or financial.

### *Harvest*

Not every personal season is one of tragedy or crisis. Some seasons—such as harvest seasons—involve reaping the rewards of our efforts. These can be times of great intensity. When the crop is ready to be reaped, it is time to work from morning to night to get the harvest in before it spoils. This is similar to Christmas season in retail, tax time in accounting, Easter in churches, finals week in college, fiscal quarter end or year end in business, or play-off time in sports. It's the championship season. It is time to push to the limit. Harvest seasons are intense times of busy, hard work—and they should be.

> When the crop is ready to be reaped, it is time to work from morning to night to get the harvest in before it spoils.

*Celebration*
Often just as intense as seasons of harvest are seasons of celebration. Graduations, engagements, anniversaries, and retirements may include parties, awards, dinners, ceremonies, and festivities—sometimes lasting several days—not to mention all the preparation that goes into making these events special.

*Business*
Workplace shifts and projects have their own rhythms and seasons. Product development comes in cycles, as does bringing a new product to market. These are not times for balance; these are times for embracing rhythm and giving everything you have to the season you're in. If you move into a new position or division in a company, a rhythm begins of forming new relationships and perhaps working in a new environment. Starting a new enterprise, such as a business, an organization, or a church, carries its own rhythm, as does shutting down an enterprise. Closure is as important a rhythm as a new beginning.

## Identify Your Personal Seasons

What personal seasons are you in right now? Kairos seasons can be difficult to identify because they are so varied and unique. It may help you to think in terms of broad categories: beginnings and endings, exertion and rest, grief and celebration. Where are you giving intense effort right now? Where are you coasting? Where are you full of joy? Where are you in pain? An ending, such as seeing your son graduate or your daughter leave for a great job in another state, can be both a time to cry and a time to rejoice.

Learning to make the most of your kairos rhythms begins with identifying your personal seasons.

Are you in an intense season, ramping up to a major fund-raising event, helping someone run for political office, or studying for the CPA exam? Are you in an "off-season," with the kids having left the nest, the holidays over, the tourists gone? Is it summer break in your life, or finals? Are you in the play-offs, preseason, or off-season? Perhaps you are in a seventh-inning stretch or at a two-minute warning, taking a brief break before an intense time of finishing. Learning to make the most of your kairos rhythms begins with identifying your personal seasons.

---

LIFE EXERCISE: *Identify the current personal seasons in your life. How does recognizing your current seasons help to put your life-management issues into perspective?*

---

## Life Stages

> *The length of our days is seventy years—or eighty, if we have the strength; yet their span is but trouble and sorrow, for they quickly pass, and we fly away. . . . Teach us to number our days aright, that we may gain a heart of wisdom.*
>
> PSALM 90:10, 12

If you are like most people, you are not fully aware of your stage of life. As a result, you may be trying to engage in activities and bear responsibilities that are not yours to handle right now. Applying the kairos rhythm strategies to your life stage can powerfully reduce your busyness and stress.

We find it amusing when we see little kids playing house, dressing up like adults, sipping tea, and playacting as if they were thirty years older. On the other hand, it's sad when children are forced to assume adult responsibilities before they are ready.

It's crazy for adults to take on expectations for an age or stage other than the one in which they are living. Students in college sometimes want to start their careers before they graduate. But that is the time for school; work will come soon enough.

Some parents make the mistake of hurrying their children to grow up. They think it's cute or cool for their preadolescent children to dress like teenagers, to fantasize about boyfriends or girlfriends. This adds unwarranted pressure to these young lives by pushing them into a stage they are not ready for.

In a serious dating relationship, teenagers may begin to act as if they are married, emotionally and socially. But they are not there yet, and trying to maintain an exclusive relationship as teenagers only adds undue stress. At any stage of life, when we take on expectations from a previous or future stage, we increase our stress, busyness, and distraction beyond what's natural. As the Bible says, "Each day has enough trouble of its own" (Matthew 6:34). Though it is wise to plan for the future, we can't live there until we get there.

Though it is wise to plan for the future, we can't live there until we get there.

In every culture, people live through stages. We are babies, then children, then teens, and then adults. We stop growing at some point and start dying. No matter how much medical science has tried to reverse the aging process, our bodies still deteriorate and decay.

Though we do not fully understand it, doctors can describe in detail how our bodies slow down and wear out. But we don't need advanced degrees to tell us that our eyes don't see as well and our ears don't hear as well as they used to.

Beyond biological changes, our life span includes stages described largely by family relationships. We begin as children living with our parents. Then, as adults, we relate to our parents differently, as we no longer depend on them for support but may still want their advice or help. Then a time comes when we begin to take care of our parents as they once cared for us. For some people, that involves significant involvement when parents can no longer drive or live alone or manage their daily needs.

Once we have children of our own, we begin another parallel cycle. After raising them in our homes, we send them out into the world, watch them get married, and then applaud them when they give birth to our grandchildren. As parents, the rhythms of our lives shift as our children grow up. Their new rhythms create ours.

**Infancy:** adapt to interrupted or little sleep; meet the needs of this new, helpless little person

**Toddlers:** begin to teach and train; kid-proof the house; constant supervision

**School age:** attend holiday plays and open houses; help with homework; morning and bedtime rituals; sports, dance, and other activities

**Teen years:** deal with adolescence and teens' increasing independence; dating; driving; first jobs

**Post-high school:** help young adults figure out what to do next—college, vocational school, job, marriage

**Empty nest:** reset rhythms until grandchildren come, then all the joys of grandparenthood

Consider the stages of your life and what different responsibilities and opportunities each future stage may call for. Until you've been through a few transitions, it's easy to assume that every stage will be like the stage you're currently in. But those who have already passed through most of the stages look back on how unique each stage was and how quickly it passed.

You kiss your newborn's head, then kiss his cheek on the first day of school, then hear about his first kiss, then kiss him goodbye as he leaves home, then hear the minister say, "You may now kiss the bride." Before you know it, you are watching him kiss his newborn's head as the cycle begins again. You hope you will be able to give your grandbaby many kisses and to live long enough to hear again, "You may now kiss the bride." Wisdom calls us to live fully in each season, without getting sidetracked by regret for a season that's past or by fear of a season yet to come.

## Studying Life Stages

Our lifetimes are a linear rhythm (nonrepeating, noncyclical) in which stages progress unrelentingly through the years. Life stages have long been recognized across all cultures, as indicated by the famous ancient riddle: What walks on four feet in the morning, two feet in the afternoon, and three feet in the evening? (Think crawling, walking, and using a cane.)

In Shakespeare's *As You Like It*, Jaques tells us that people live through seven stages in his "all the world's a stage" speech:

*All the world's a stage,*
*And all the men and women merely players:*

*They have their exits and their entrances;*
*And one man in his time plays many parts,*
*His acts being seven ages.*[7]

The first psychologist to view life by stages was Else Frenkel-Brunswick. Her conclusion that every person passes through five phases anticipated the life cycle articulated by Erik Erikson. With the publication of *Childhood and Society* in 1950, Erikson first made the concept of life stages popular. For him, each stage of adulthood is associated with a specific psychological struggle that shapes us.[8]

Fuller Theological Seminary professor Robert Clinton's classic book *The Making of a Leader* popularized the concept of life stages in leadership theory. His studies of biblical and modern leaders have now been extended through the work of doctoral students to an ever-widening range of people. The studies confirm that leaders develop through identifiable stages. Clinton encourages building a time line to envision how God has worked and will likely work to shape a person over time.

> Wisdom calls us to live fully in each season, without getting sidetracked by regret for a season that's past or by fear of a season yet to come.

No one, however, has done more to advance and popularize the study of life stages than Gail Sheehy. In her groundbreaking book *Passages*, Sheehy identifies major stages that most adults live through in their twenties, thirties, and forties.

Sheehy explains that after childhood we "continue to develop by stages and to confront predictable crises, or passages between each stage of adulthood."[9] Almost twenty years after *Passages*, Sheehy wrote *New Passages*, about a "second adulthood" in midlife. In *New Passages*, Sheehy extends her work on life stages to the decades past the age of fifty. In the introduction, Sheehy summarizes the point of her first book:

> *Passages* helped to popularize an entirely new concept: that adulthood continues to proceed by stages of development throughout the life cycle. Unlike childhood stages, the stages of adult life are characterized not by physical growth but by steps in psychological and social growth. Marriage, childbirth, first job, empty nest are what we call *marker events*, the concrete happenings of our lives. A developmental stage, however, is not defined by marker events; it is defined by an underlying *impulse toward change* that signals us from the realm of mind or spirit. This inner realm is where we register the *meaning* of our participation in the external world: How do we *feel* about our job, family roles, social roles? In what ways are our values, goals, and aspirations being invigorated or violated by our present life structure? How many parts of our personality can we live out, and what parts are we leaving out?[10]

Though Sheehy focuses on the crisis, the *passage*, that moves a person from one stage to another, she also describes well what is happening in each stage. This is where I see value for a rhythmic life. Identify your current life stage, and then "ride the wave" of your life stage by asking, What expectations can you release? What opportunities can you seize? And what's next—what joys can you embrace and what hopes can you anticipate? Sheehy's summary of adult life stages is interesting and insightful.

Sheehy believes there is now a revolution in the human life cycle. Puberty arrives earlier by several years than it did at the turn of the twentieth century. Adolescence is prolonged until the late twenties for the middle class, the midtwenties for blue-collar men and women. Middle age is extended. She says, "Fifty is now what forty used to be."[11]

> What expectations can you release? What opportunities can you seize? What joys can you embrace? What hopes can you anticipate?

In *New Passages*, Sheehy presents three broad stages: Provisional Adulthood (ages eighteen to thirty), First Adulthood (thirty to forty-five), and Second Adulthood (forty-five to eighty-five plus). "Each presents its own struggles and begs for a new dream," Sheehy says. She divides the Second Adulthood into two phases, the Age of Mastery (forty-five to sixty-five) and the Age of Integrity (sixty-five to eighty-five and beyond).

Frankly, I hate to be categorized. I like to think of myself as unique, an individual. Don't tell me how I'm going to be in each decade. Sheehy acknowledges that feeling, commenting, "We all have an aversion to generalities, thinking that they violate what is unique about ourselves. Yet the older we grow, the more we become aware of the commonality of our lives."[12]

Our concern is to learn how to live in time with the natural kairos rhythms of our lives. How can we ride the waves well so that we avoid crashing into the ocean bottom and instead glide onto the beach? Each stage or wave is unique, but principles for riding the waves can apply to all of them.

## Physical Health through Our Life Stages

Aging is often difficult. We tend to move through life passages as crises, both losing the blessing we enjoyed in the previous stage and being overwhelmed by the new challenges of the coming stage. Our bodies will not do what we once willed them to do.

Throughout our lives, we should be attentive to the health of the bodies that God entrusted to us. Dr. Kenneth Cooper and Dr. Tyler Cooper have written an excellent book on quality of life: *Start Strong, Finish Strong.* We know we deteriorate as we age, starting at about age twenty-five. This includes loss of bone mass, lower energy levels, loss of muscle mass, decline in aerobic capacity, impaired physical functioning, weakened immune system, loss of mental function, and reduced life span.

The Coopers compiled figures based on more than ten thousand men and women, whose histories are on file at the Cooper Clinic. And they were amazed at what they found: "Even though time and chance eventually overtake us all, a number of studies have revealed that only about a third of the natural processes of aging are beyond our influence. In other words, about *two-thirds* of that steady deterioration of mental acuity, physical strength, and stamina can be *slowed, stopped—or even reversed.*"[13]

The Coopers recommend seven simple steps that they believe can enable you to extend your life span by ten to twenty *quality* years:

Step #1: Quit putting off that gold-standard physical;

Step #2: Launch a realistic fitness plan;

Step #3: Begin eating a longevity diet;

Step #4: Follow a wise supplement strategy;

Step #5: Do serious smoke control;

Step #6: Counteract creeping substance abuse; and

Step #7: Engage in effective mind-spirit practices.[14]

Our health needs will change over time. What we need to be healthy at age twelve is not the same as what we need at age fifty-seven. Our eating and exercise habits should change as we move through life's stages. What we do to stay healthy physically varies with our life stage.

## Identify Your Life Stage

Knowing your life stage enables you to ride the kairos wave that is before you right now. It helps you avoid trying to ride a wave that has gone by or one that is still on the horizon. Let's not try to live as if we have an empty nest until the kids are gone; and once they've left home, let's not try to keep rearing them.

Identify your current stage so you can apply rhythm strategies to your present life, and then identify the next stage you will likely enter. You might even be in the midst of a passage between stages, as I am (moving from the child-rearing years to an empty nest).

Identify your current stage so you can apply rhythm strategies to your present life, and then identify the next stage you will likely enter.

Three major elements will help you identify your current life stage: your biological age, family relationships, and major multi-year phases. Some of these stages may begin with a crisis.

First, how old are you? It makes a difference whether you are reading this book as a nineteen-year-old, a forty-nine-year-old, or a sixty-nine-year-old—three very different life stages. Biologically, are you in puberty, in child-bearing years, or past menopause? Are you at the peak of fitness and strength or in the time of physical decline?

Second, identify your family relationships. Are you single, never married? married? divorced? remarried? Are you pregnant?

Do you have children? stepchildren? grandchildren? Are your children at home, or do you have an empty nest? Have they left and boomeranged back? Are you caring for aging parents, or are your parents still caring for you? Usually, having a baby, getting married, or getting divorced shifts you into a new stage of life.

Third, are you in a new, multi-year phase? An example might be a move to a new place that creates a geographic shift and may take you to a new stage.

Changes at work can move you to a new stage, especially if it is a change to a new career in a different field, or from being employed by a company to being self-employed. Changes in service or education can usher in a new stage of life. Entering active military duty or starting studies as a full-time student will create a new stage of life.

Sometimes a health crisis will generate a new life stage. Losing a significant amount of weight can transform you into a new person. If you suffer a major disability, you may enter a new stage of limited mobility. If you find out you have cancer or AIDS, you enter a new stage of life, as does your primary caregiver.

> Understanding the two basic kinds of kairos rhythms—personal seasons and life stages—gives us a foundation for learning how to live our lives in rhythm.

Our youngest child will graduate from high school in 2009. By 2013, if he's on track, he should be finishing college. So, over the next several years, my wife and I will move into entirely new stages of life—from parents with kids at home to parents with kids at college to parents with a truly empty nest. Our current stage of raising teenagers, which started in 1997, will end in 2010 when the youngest turns twenty.

When you know what "time" it is in your life, you have a basis for figuring out how to live well in that unique time of life. The three kairos rhythm strategies show you how to live well in each different stage of life.

Understanding the two basic kinds of kairos rhythms—personal seasons and life stages—gives us a foundation for learning how to live our lives in rhythm. In the next few chapters, we will explore how to release false expectations that don't fit your current rhythm, seize unique opportunities in your current kairos seasons, and anticipate what lies ahead in seasons and stages to come.

Once you can identify the waves, you can discover how to ride them well. Using the three kairos rhythm strategies, you coast with peace by releasing false expectations that don't fit your current rhythm, you ride with fulfillment by seizing unique opportunities this kairos season offers you, and you find hope in anticipating the waves that still lie ahead of you.

---

LIFE EXERCISE: *Identify your current life stage and the next one to come.*

*My current life stage is . . .*

*When did it start? When will it likely end? What are the particular stresses, blessings, and opportunities of this life stage?*

*My next life stage will likely be . . .*

*How will this stage differ from the one I'm in?*

# 6
# Kairos Strategy #1: Release Expectations

*God, grant me the serenity to accept the things*
*I cannot change.*

REINHOLD NIEBUHR, "THE SERENITY PRAYER"

Guilt haunts us all. Some of it is deserved—we've messed up and we need to confess, apologize, and do what we can to make amends. A lot of our guilty feelings, however, are self-imposed and unnecessary. We sometimes feel guilty for things that are beyond our control or not our fault. We feel guilty because of expectations we have about what we ought to be doing or not doing during a particular season of our lives. Or we still feel guilty about things we've confessed and for which we've already received forgiveness. If we can learn how to release these false feelings of guilt, we can live more peaceful and productive lives.

Peace comes from living fully in each season, without getting sidetracked by resentment for the current season or regret for a season gone by or fear of a season yet to come. Identify the life stage you are in right now, and determine to live in that stage and not in any other stage, past or future. I see married folks wishing they were single, singles rushing to be married, parents resenting the burdens of raising children, and infertile women longing to bear a child. Young people wish they were older, and older people wish they were younger. These are all examples of trying to live in a different season than the one they're in. Not that it's wrong to hope for a mate or a child, but we each have a life to live now.

When we grasp the wisdom of living our lives in rhythm, we will learn to be fully present in our current season and stage. We will not envy someone who is in another stage or try to hang on to a stage we have already left or try to live in a season that is yet to come. Peace is life giving: "A heart at peace gives life to the body, but envy rots the bones" (Proverbs 14:30).

Writing from a Roman prison, the apostle Paul said, "I have learned to be content whatever the circumstances" (Philippians 4:11). As we learn to practice releasing expectations, we will grow in contentment. Peace and contentment come from trusting that we are right where God wants us. Peace is an aspiration expressed in the famous "Serenity Prayer," which is offered in twelve-step meetings all over the world.

When we grasp the wisdom of living our lives in rhythm, we will learn to be fully present in our current season and stage.

Many kairos events are out of our control. When they happen, how will we respond? We can do more than grudgingly accept them; we can understand them and embrace them.

Releasing expectations and embracing rhythm means we accept the limitations placed on us by certain seasons. For instance, when we are in a season of grief, it is not the time to start a large project. When rehabilitating an injury, don't start a step-aerobics class. While on vacation, don't plan to get work done—relax. When it's crunch time to get the product out the door, don't expect to have significant family time.

By releasing expectations that don't fit your current rhythms, you will reduce feelings of guilt. By trusting that God has you in this season and stage, you will experience increased peace. It's valuable to consider both personal stages and life stages. The following examples help you see how you could release expectations in your personal seasons.

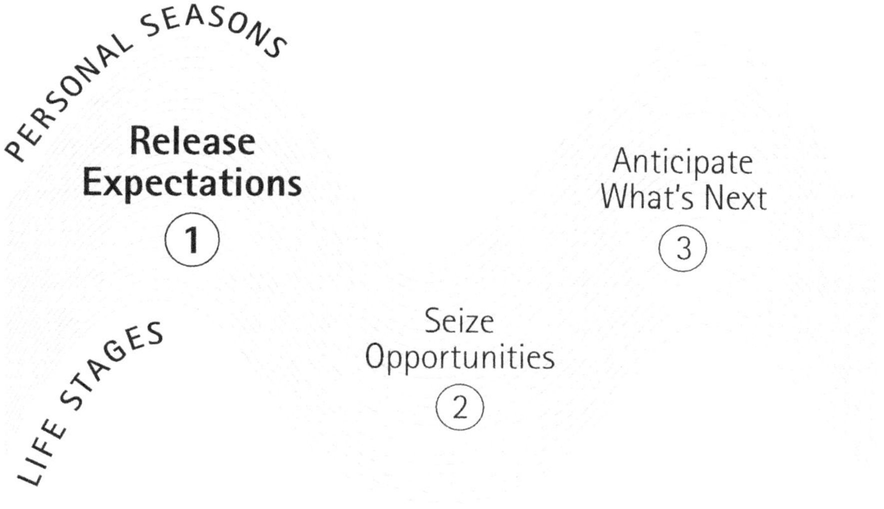


## Releasing Expectations in Personal Seasons

If you are in a close relationship, it is vital to appreciate not only your own personal seasons but also the seasons your loved one is experiencing.

## MARIE'S MISCARRIAGE TEARS

Marie called me at the encouragement of a friend who knew she was hurting. She and her husband, Hector, were happy about her being pregnant, but she was much more excited than he was. They picked out names. She practiced good prenatal health habits and talked with her boss about her job.

Then, at five months, she lost the baby. The miscarriage devastated her. Weeks later, she would still burst out crying at the oddest times. Hector was frustrated with her, telling her to get it together. Marie felt guilty for still grieving. She was trying to avoid the guilt by going right back to work and flinging herself into projects.

When you have suffered a significant loss, it is okay to hurt, to be angry, to blame God. That is all part of the normal process.

I encouraged her to take time to grieve well. When you have suffered a significant loss, it is okay to hurt, to be angry, to blame God. That is all part of the normal process. Just don't get stuck in one phase of the cycle. Marie was able to release herself from the false expectation that everything should go back to normal right after the miscarriage, or even within the first several months. She released the expectations that she wouldn't cry and that she could work as hard and accomplish as much as usual while she was grieving.

For the sake of their marriage, Hector needed to understand the rhythm of Marie's grief. At a secondary level, he too was walking through grief—perhaps a less intense and shorter season, but it was important for him to acknowledge his own feelings as well. If you are working through significant grief, release the expectations that you should be bouncing right back and capable of starting a big new enterprise. You may need some time off or a reduced schedule for a while. Emotionally release yourself from the expectation of "getting back to normal" right away.

## DIVORCE'S ANGER

Divorce begins an unfortunately common cycle. In our church, we host the national DivorceCare ministry. Dozens of people have told me what a difference this one-semester course made for them. Why? Because it delves into the rhythm of divorce, the predictable patterns that couples and individuals experience when they get divorced. Immediately after a divorce, release yourself from the expectation of a new relationship. This is not the time to date. And release yourself from the expectation that you will "get over it" quickly.

The standard advice is that it takes about one year for every four years of marriage to recover from the devastation of divorce. Release the expectation that you will not be angry. Anger is a natural part of grief. You don't want to get stuck in anger, but it is a false expectation to assume that you will avoid anger because you are having an "amicable" divorce. After (or while) you work through your natural feelings of anger, it's good to forgive your former spouse and to seek to work things out peacefully.

When it is time to vacation, take the time to really rest and rejuvenate; let go of expectations that you will also be working.

## REALLY RESTING ON VACATION

Not all personal seasons have negative expectations to release. When it is time to vacation, take the time to really rest and rejuvenate; let go of expectations that you will also be working some proportion of the time (that's the old balance model). This is your time to renew.

John has achieved success and advancement at his job because he has worked harder than most everyone around him. Often he is the first to arrive and the last to leave. It's not uncommon to receive an e-mail from John time-stamped 11:30 p.m. or 5:00 a.m. He is always "on," solving problems, creating new ideas, pushing initiatives forward. The BlackBerry never leaves his side. He has been ranked number one in the division more often than anyone else in the last five years.

On vacation, his wife, Jessica, threatened to throw the BlackBerry in the pool. She was sick of hearing the silly ring tone, and it hardly made things better in silent mode because John still took the calls. Even over dinner, he was texting under the table, as if she wouldn't notice. Oblivious to her feelings, John did not realize that his work obsession was about to wreck his marriage. When you are on vacation, vacate work. Seize the opportunity for re-creation. This is the time to invest in relationships, grow in intimacy, and build connections with those you love. This is the time to get off the grid—don't answer e-mail or respond to voice mail. Leave the BlackBerry at home; don't bring the laptop. Resist the urge to check in. Lounge by the pool. Have long, leisurely dinners.

### TAMARA AND HER MOM'S LAST DAYS

Sometimes your season is generated by what's happening to someone very close to you. When my wife, Tamara, was in her twenties, she and her brother and sister had the privilege of caring for their mom while she was dying of lung cancer. As an energetic and gifted lady, Tamara was involved in many activities at church at the time, in addition to raising our young children. She felt overwhelmed, yet she also felt that she needed to care for her mom while remaining engaged in all these other activities.

A wise older lady, Linda Cole, told her, "Tamara, relax. This is your time to care for your mom. All the rest will wait." That was what Tamara needed to hear. It was her season to care for her mom. She found peace by releasing the false expectations that she should still lead the children's choir and teach a Bible study.

If you are caring for an ill, disabled, or dying relative, this is not your season to run a marathon. It's not your time to be president of the booster club. If you just got married, it's not the time to start a new business.

### CATHY'S CHEMO

Brandon and Cathy have become closer friends as we have walked with them through Cathy's breast cancer treatments. Before the chemo started, Cathy was a regular volunteer at the hospital. A deeply compassionate person, she had always given to others and enjoyed helping other people in their times of need. Now, flat on her back, she had no energy, and she could not even drive her car.

We organized friends from church to bring them meals, and though she was appreciative, she felt bad because she could do nothing in return. It was embarrassing and uncomfortable for her.

We can release so much guilt and frustration if we simply realize what time it is in our lives and live in time with that particular rhythm.

Tamara had the opportunity to share Linda Cole's advice with Cathy: "This is your time to receive help. There will be another time to give." She encouraged Cathy to let go of the expectation that she should be returning the favor or helping others at this time. She needed to drop a false sense of guilt and relax in the peace of knowing that this was her time to heal, to endure the effects of the chemotherapy in order to treat the cancer.

We can release so much guilt and frustration if we simply realize what time it is in our lives and live in time with that particular rhythm, without trying to take on another rhythm that doesn't fit our present situation. Trying to maintain old rhythms while taking on new ones is discordant living. It only creates emotional noise in our lives.

### MIKE JONES'S OVERFULL LIFE

Remember Mike Jones, who was trying to have it all—the perfect suburban life—by balancing everything right now? He needs to realize what season he is in and release some expectations. For instance, it's soccer season for his daughter, and Mike is helping to coach her team. During soccer season, Mike would find more peace by releasing the expectation that he should also be playing in a men's basketball league.

In Mike's neighborhood, the home owners compete each month for "best yard." Mike is frustrated because the neighbors across the street always have such a nice yard. But those neighbors are a retired couple who devote themselves to their yard. It's their hobby. Why is Mike even trying to compete at this season of his life? He should release the expectation that he should enter the "best yard" competition. He should let it go, drop the unnecessary guilt, and cheer on his daughter on Saturday mornings without worrying about the yard. If anything, he should have soccer goals in the yard, not landscaping with boulders or lovely flowers. There will be another stage, later in life, when Mike can garden with his wife and try to win the "best yard" prize.

### DAVID DURING FINALS WEEK

Short, intense seasons can be excessively stressful if we try to be "balanced" during those times. At Georgia Tech during final exams, my son David does not sleep much. He does not call home. Downtime has almost no place in his schedule those few days. No parties, no hanging out with friends. He has dropped the expectation that he will be out having fun with his frat brothers that week. But David is at peace because he knows that this is not the time for relaxing. During finals, he is not trying to balance all his obligations. This is crunch time. As a result, he has less frustration and stress.

In work environments, we need to pay attention to the season. In our global awareness, we need to be cognizant of rhythms in other cultures around the world. During the Chinese New Year celebration, the whole country of China takes a two-week break. It is not the time for the Chinese to do business. You will frustrate yourself trying to get things done in Europe during August. That is the time for family holidays, not for business transactions. When the sea is calm, don't resent the lack of waves. Relax. The stormy, adventurous waves are coming again soon enough.

## Releasing Expectations in Life Stages

This same strategy of releasing expectations applies powerfully in the longer life stages. In fact, I find life stages to be the kairos rhythm that offers the greatest opportunity to dismiss false guilt. If we would only recognize our life stage and release expectations that don't fit our current stage, we would find so much more peace. Perhaps one of the following examples touches on a similar situation in your life, showing you where you can release expectations that don't fit your current life stage.

> When the sea is calm, don't resent the lack of waves. Relax.

### FIXED INCOME

If you are retired and on a limited income, stop trying to spend like you did in the days when you had your highest income at the peak of your career. Release the expectation that you should still have that income. You are in a new season now that does not include stock bonuses for exceeding the annual goal. Let go of the expectation that your charitable contributions can continue at the same level.

### VICTOR AND SUZANNE'S EARLY MARRIAGE

In their early twenties, Victor and Suzanne were just getting started in entry-level jobs as a bank teller and a kindergarten teacher. As they moved toward getting married, they looked for a place to live—a nice enough place, by their middle-class, suburban standards. Then they went shopping for furniture, a flat-screen TV, housewares, appliances, and stuff to decorate their place. They bought two cars and signed up for cable TV, cell phone service, and Internet access. And they bought a dog. Before they knew it, they were drowning in debt. Still, it was easy for Victor to feel guilty that he couldn't afford all the things Suzanne had had growing up.

That's unnecessary guilt. Victor and Suzanne need to release the false expectation that they should fill their apartment with all the material possessions their parents have in their homes. This is their getting-started season. If the income isn't there to support this lifestyle without going into debt, they should release the expectation to have two cars, a golden retriever, and Dish Network. They shouldn't use credit to get these things before they have the funds to do so.

> Be at peace with the stage God has you in right now. Release your expectations of other times, and stop envying others who are older or younger.

Young people tend to be in a hurry to get to the next stage. Young children long to be older. When they are nine, they want to be thirteen, with all the perceived advantages of being older, such as a later bedtime and fewer restrictions on video games and movies. In junior high, they long to be in high school; in high school, they long to get out into the "real world." When they're eighteen, they want to be twenty-one and recognized as an adult. Ironically, as they get older, they'll start wishing they were younger.

Be at peace with the stage God has you in right now. Release your expectations of other times, and stop envying others who are older or younger. When we have little, we wish for more, we long to be wealthy. After we get more, we resent all the hassles, complexities, clutter, and anxieties that go along with having more. We wish for a simpler life. Instead, we should adapt to the rhythm of the season we're in and make the most of the lives we have—not the lives we wish we had.

### OVERWHELMING LAUNDRY

Early in our marriage and our child-rearing years, when Tamara was overwhelmed by the amount of laundry she had to do—not to mention keeping up the rest of the house and caring for the kids while I was at work or school—she asked her friend Linda, who had six kids of her own, "What do you do about the piles of laundry?" Linda replied, "When it gets to be too much, I throw it in a room and shut the door." Her point was that, at this life stage, Tamara needed to release the false expectation that she could keep up with the laundry. That advice was so freeing to Tamara. Years later, she still smiles remembering the guilt that fell away when she released herself from the expectation that there would be no piles of dirty laundry.

### BART'S NAVY YEARS

The strategy of releasing expectations also applies when you are young and single. Sometimes guilt comes from comparing your rhythm with someone else's. My son Bart served in the U.S. Navy for four years after high school. When the time came to go on to college, he was twenty-three years old. By that time, some of his old high school friends were finishing college and starting their careers. My son could have become frustrated with himself or felt guilty that he was just starting college, but that would have been taking on another person's rhythm. Instead, just as he had given himself fully to his service in the Navy, now it was time to focus on earning a degree. The season for starting his career will come soon enough, after he finishes his time in college. By fully investing himself in his current season, Bart will make the most of his time in school and avoid feelings of false guilt.

> Sometimes guilt comes from comparing your rhythm with someone else's.

### JANE'S MAGAZINE

Remember Jane, who was struggling to "balance" her magazine as well as all the issues in her personal life? As Jane and I talked about her stage of life (parenting young children) and her season of life (caring for her dying stepfather), she decided to drastically reduce the frequency of her magazine issues. Rather than publishing an issue every other month, she decided to publish twice a year. Releasing herself from that self-imposed expectation instantly relieved her guilt, and a new peace poured over her as she devoted her attention appropriately to her stepfather and her kids.

### BEING A DAD

A key discovery for me was realizing what a short time I have left to raise my children compared to how long I will be in the next life stage—empty nest to retirement. I was in my late thirties when I realized I had only about fourteen years left to raise my kids, but many years after that to do other things. That insight made me seriously re-evaluate my commitments and my expectations of myself, both conscious and unconscious. I asked myself, "What can I do only in this stage?"

Several years ago, a man I respect invited me to serve on the board of his organization. I accepted. A short time later, I re-evaluated my priorities and commitments and realized I had many years ahead when I could serve on boards, but only a few more years to raise my kids. I realized *I* had chosen to accept an invitation to serve on a board but that *God* had made me the father of my five children. Others could serve on the board, but no one could replace me as father to my kids. After one year, I resigned from the board and dropped the expectation that I should serve on boards at this stage in my life.

## TEARS LEAVING WACO

As stages shift, we must release the expectations of the stage we are leaving and embrace the new realities of the emerging stage. As we grow older, we tend to want to hold on to the good things from the life stage we are leaving. Last August, it was a joy to take my only daughter off to college at Baylor University in Waco, Texas. But after getting everything settled in her dorm room, as I was driving away, tears streamed down my face. I knew she would no longer be living at home.

As stages shift, we must release the expectations of the stage we are leaving and embrace the new realities of the emerging stage.

Those were appropriate tears; but if I had turned around and driven back to Baylor to insist that my daughter come back to live at home, I would have been grasping at the remnants of an old life stage that was now gone. In this new life stage and personal season, both my daughter and I needed to release the expectation that she will live at home just as she did when she was growing up. If we don't release the expectations of previous stages, we inhibit our ability to receive the blessings in the new stage that's beginning. William Blake expresses the idea of releasing in his poem "Eternity."

*He who binds to himself a joy,*
*Does the winged life destroy;*
*But he who kisses the joy as it flies*
*Lives in eternity's sun rise.*[1]

Release the expectation that blessings from one stage can always be carried to the next stage of life.

### AGING GRACEFULLY

Older people struggle with losing the strength of youth. Some try excessive exercise, rigorous diets, and exotic remedies in order to regain their vigor. Nothing is wrong with healthy living and staying in shape, but trying to regain bygone youth is a losing battle that will yield only frustration and eventual failure. The next battle is even harder—accepting the often-gradual loss of independence.

> Trying to regain bygone youth is a losing battle that will yield only frustration and eventual failure.

My dad is trying to release the expectation that his body will do today what it did yesterday. No longer is he going to run down the track to the finish line, ski down the slope at high speeds, or dive deep underwater with his scuba gear. He can choose to stay frustrated and live with guilt that he is not running like he used to run, but that is unnecessary stress.

### NEW MOTHERHOOD

When I shared the concept of releasing expectations with the Mom's-Day-Out staff, I mentioned that I so often see new moms with little children trying to keep up with their girlfriends—single or married—who don't have kids. New moms, I said, feel obligated to keep going to the gym, doing lengthy Bible studies, and serving all over the church. They laughed nervously.

Then I told them, "This is not your time for long workouts or involved Bible studies. This is your time to raise your babies. Release yourself from false expectations that don't fit this new life stage. This is the time for mommy-and-me exercise or walks with the stroller. Bite-size devotionals fit the bill instead of serious studies." The relief was visible on their faces. Here was a pastor giving them permission to do less Bible study and church service and to focus on what was most important during that crucial life stage—raising their kids.

What about your life? Do you need to set yourself free from unnecessary guilt to discover more peace in your life? As you consider your current personal seasons and life stage—your kairos rhythms—what expectations could you release?

---

**LIFE EXERCISE:** *Make a list, beginning with the following phrase: "I will release the following expectations . . ."*

# 7
# Kairos Strategy #2: Seize Opportunities

*For such a time as this . . .*

ESTHER 4:14

*Make the most of every opportunity.*

COLOSSIANS 4:5

You can live full-out without burning out. One of the keys to finding fulfillment is to seize unique opportunities within your current kairos rhythms. When it's play-off time, go full-out to win. When it's the off-season, rest and rebuild your capacity. When you are young, with more energy, use it. When you are older and have more wisdom, share it. To carry out your life's mission, seize the opportunities that are evident or latent in your current life stage and seasons.

By fulfillment, I am not referring to self-actualization or some superficial psychological state of well-being. Rather, fulfillment is the carrying out of your life's mission. It is being a responsible steward in each stage of your life.

Burnout comes from trying to seize opportunities that do not fit the current season of your life; it is created by trying to meet unreleased false expectations. I am often guilty of taking on more than I should. One personality profile told me I was prone to "get too many irons in the fire." It was right. I do.

Does that mean we should stop setting ambitious goals? Bob Biehl wrote a book titled *Stop Setting Goals If You Would Rather Solve Problems*. Though the title is obviously provocative, the point is well taken. Goal setting is wise, but we cannot predict what tomorrow will bring. It may bring a huge opportunity for which we haven't set a goal. We need to be prepared to seize the opportunities that come our way in each stage and season of life.

> Goal setting is wise, but we cannot predict what tomorrow will bring.

Life is not a calm lake; it's more like a wild ocean. We encounter unexpected waves. Some we're able to ride; others turn us upside down and crash us into the sand. It is not that we should avoid setting goals but that our goals should be set only with a vivid understanding of our life's rhythms.

## Esther's Kairos Moment

The ancient story of Esther portrays a young Hebrew woman who was chosen to be a concubine for King Xerxes of Persia. Though her situation was obviously not ideal, one she would not have chosen, she was in the palace and able to communicate with King Xerxes at a crucial time for the survival of her people. Haman, a powerful figure in the court, acting out of anger and hurt pride, had plotted to purge all the Jews from the land. Esther's uncle, Mordecai, challenged her to step up, saying that perhaps God had put her in Xerxes' palace *"for such a time as this."*

Be alert for "such a time as this" kind of moments. How could you seize the opportunities that your current stage or season provides you? For instance, when recovering from an injury or accident, you may have weeks off from work. Though physically limited, you have an opportunity to read books you've always wanted to read, to enjoy long conversations with friends, and to take extended times of prayer to connect deeply with God.

You've heard the classic advice that experienced parents tell new parents: "They're only babies for such a short time. Treasure these days." And young parents should. When you have babies, you get to hold them and snuggle them—but that season doesn't last. Babies become toddlers, who become kindergartners, who become squirrelly sixth graders, who become teenagers. We need to seize the unique opportunities granted by each season and stage of our lives and embrace the blessings in those opportunities. Seize with gusto what God has put before you right now. You will find personal fulfillment and joy in living your mission in this particular time, no matter what it is.

Look for the blessings available at this time in your life. My dad could resent that he no longer has the physical stamina to do dentistry all day or to run a 10K race. Instead, he chooses to focus on the joy of painting with watercolors, a newfound pursuit that he did not have time for earlier in his life.

Look for the blessings available at this time in your life.

We increase our stress when we don't count our blessings. We breed unhappiness and discontentment when we live with regret and resentment for what we can't have, or wish we didn't have. When we resent babies for their intrusion into our peaceful lives, or teenagers for their boisterousness, we risk missing out on the once-in-a-lifetime opportunities those life stages afford us.

## Gratitude Is a Powerful Stimulant

Pay attention to the juice in the half-full glass, not the emptiness in the other half. Even in tough times there are blessings to enjoy. If you choose to, you can find joy even in the midst of poverty and heartache. Funerals bring families together like nothing else does. Memories and stories come pouring out as family members gather to grieve, remember, and honor their loved one.

Each season carries with it distinct benefits and challenges. We waste our lives when we fixate on the difficulties and neglect to seize the opportunities and enjoy the blessings. Married couples resent the obligations of marriage and wish they were as free as singles. Singles resent their loneliness and wish for a life partner. Empty nesters feel empty, and parents of preschoolers feel exhausted. And yet each season brings special joys to be cherished.

Older people wish they could regain the strength and beauty of youth. Younger people wish for the wisdom and wealth of their elders. People living in the country may resent the restrictions of small-town life and wish for the excitement of the big city. Meanwhile, city dwellers are longing to see the stars at night and to enjoy the quiet of nature far away from the hum of traffic. Enjoy the opportunities and blessings of your current season. They may not carry over into what comes next. Live fully in this present season without resenting its challenges, demanding the next season to start now, or pining over a season gone by.

## Seize Opportunities in Personal Seasons

Right now I am at a lake house, alone for a precious two and a half days to write. I must seize this time. I intend to write all I can while I am apart from the rest of my regular world. I want to make the most of it.

When it is your time—whatever that time may be—go for it. When dove season opens, the fields are full of hunters trying to get their limit. When play-off time comes in sports, the teams who have made the grade know that the time has come to turn it up a notch. Nobody wants to go "one and done." Now is the time for everyone to give it their best, their all. It's time to sacrifice and go the extra mile. It's time to seize the opportunity before it passes you by.

We often use sports analogies in our culture because they're easy to understand, but these same principles apply in other areas of life as well. For instance, Christmastime is harvesttime in retail sales. A good retailer will seize the opportunity to earn as much in December as possible, knowing that business will slow down after the first of the year. Every business has its seasons when extra time and energy are required to make the most of an opportunity. Focusing our efforts during these peak times will often pay off with maximized results—results we can never achieve if we miss the strategic kairos moments.

It's important to see how these kairos rhythm strategies flow together. There's an opportune time for releasing expectations, just as there is an opportune time for seizing opportunities. But if we're trying to keep everything "balanced," we may miss the kairos opportunities that come our way.

If we're trying to keep everything "balanced," we may miss the kairos opportunities that come our way.

Seizing opportunities is as important on vacation as it is on the job. For instance, John and Jessica will have a better vacation if they release expectations of working during their time away. This is their time to seize the opportunity to build a deeper relationship and renew their strength. So often, people return from their vacations exhausted. It has become cliché to say, "I need a vacation from my vacation." People who don't release expectations and seize opportunities on their vacations will reap further dissipation of energy rather than renewal and rejuvenation.

On your vacation, do what restores you—and *enjoy* doing it. Nap. Read a book. Take long walks. Go on an adventure. Experience an extreme sport. Ride a roller coaster. Rent a mountain bike. Focus on your loved ones. Play eighteen holes of golf—or thirty-six, if you're up to it. Build sand castles with the kids. Hike the trails at a leisurely pace, relishing the tiny flowers and the towering peaks. See the sites and hit the streets. Play as hard as you work.

## ROGER'S BURNOUT

Even in seemingly bad seasons, there are opportunities to seize and blessings to enjoy. When I talked with Roger and his wife,

Kathryn, at their kitchen table about Roger's burnout and panic attacks, they were determined to fix the problem and get back to a "normal, balanced life" as soon as possible. Their hope was that Roger's appointment with a therapist would provide an immediate solution.

Instead, I encouraged them to seize the unique, latent opportunities in this time of emotional recovery. Roger could spend more time with his children; read novels he has not allowed himself to read; work in the garden. This could be a time to breathe deeply and take the rare opportunity to really slow down and connect with God.

What unique opportunities can be seized in a time of recovery or rehabilitation? This can be your time to read those classic books you have wanted to read for years. You can catch up with old friends. You can rest deeply, replenishing and renewing yourself, body, mind, and spirit. Too often we view rehabilitation as a negative time, making it as short as possible in order to get back to work. We resist the limitations of these times rather than seizing the opportunities. You have time in a longer season of recovery to think deeply about your life, who you are, and where you are going. Without that time, you might never have the opportunity to truly stop and reflect.

What unique opportunities can be seized in a time of recovery or rehabilitation?

### BART IN THE NAVY

Sometimes seasons are very focused, excluding all aspects of life except the one right in front of you. When my oldest son entered the Great Lakes Naval Training Center, he began a unique rhythm that excluded almost everything but "Yes, sir, Petty Officer!" The days started with intense physical training, long before the sun rose. Other aspects of Bart's life were pushed aside for the time being. Without understanding the special rhythms of basic training, one might think a new sailor's life is far out of balance. Instead, he is actually doing well in this unique rhythm. The same is true of soldiers on deployment. Their rhythm on the battlefield is demanding and far different from a college student's rhythms.

When you are on active duty, it is time to seize the unique opportunities of that unusual time. Form lasting friendships with fellow soldiers. Experience parts of the world you may never see again. Learn discipline. Get in serious physical shape.

### REDUCTION IN FORCE

The phrase *reduction in force*, or RIF, is a politically correct way of saying, "You're fired." The dreaded "pink slip" can send people spiraling into depression. It is tough to be out of work; few of us are financially prepared for it.

Use the strategy of seizing opportunities to make the most of the time you have after a job loss.

The day you are let go begins a personal season, a kairos rhythm. Typically, people go through a common pattern of emotions: disbelief, anger, fighting against it, initial elation at the free time, depression, and then a surge of effort to seek the next opportunity.

To live rhythmically in this season, you must identify the time between jobs as a kairos wave and plan how you will ride it. First, release the expectation that you will be able to continue life as it was when you were employed. Not everything will change, but many things will. Use the strategy of seizing opportunities to make the most of the time you have. Could this be an opportunity to rethink the trajectory of your life or make a career shift? Could this be a blessing in disguise, giving you the push you need for a new start, even in a new place? It is foolish to ignore or downplay the difficult emotions. You need to feel them. But it is wise to look for blessings to embrace. How will you invest the new discretionary time you have been granted?

### DAN WITH HIS TEAM AT WORK

In business, there are times of high stress when you are pressing hard to get a project finished. At the Fortune 500 company where Dan is a manager, he leads his team to give it their all when deadlines are bearing down. Dan has learned to embrace a season of hard work, to enjoy the adrenaline rush of turning the project in right before the deadline.

Rather than resenting intense seasons, enjoy the feeling of accomplishment, of pushing yourself to the limit—whether it's to write the legal brief, repair the roof, clean the house before the party, make the big sale, or finish the presentation. Seize the opportunity to accomplish something.

After Dan's team has met a deadline, they celebrate. After they've stayed up all night to finish an important project, they go out for breakfast and cheer each other on. Whatever your challenge is, take time to enjoy the accomplishment. Reward the team. Take some time off together. If you are in charge, give everyone some extra time off.

### LEROY'S CHURCH PLANT

A few months ago, a friend named Leroy Armstrong asked my advice about planting a church south of Dallas. Starting an enterprise from scratch is hard work. He's rallying everyone to help out, working a second job, and living on less than a livable salary. His wife is working more than she would like, but she and Leroy have agreed that the cause is worth it. Life for the Armstrongs is moving at a rapid pace, and every minute is filled. The church meets in a rented movie theater. Every Sunday morning, the church has to set up and take down everything. The pace is demanding. And the church plant must thrive to survive. If it stays small, it will die. Stress is high.

As I reflected on the earlier season of starting our church years, I found myself wishing I had enjoyed those days more. Starts are crazy and chaotic. You don't have things figured out; systems are not in place.

It was early fall of 1995 when I felt God calling me to start a church in McKinney, Texas. This was a one-of-a-kind spiritual experience for me. At that time, McKinney's population was only about thirty thousand, but it was growing rapidly and soon would be named the fastest-growing city of its size in America.

After eighteen months of prayer and preparation, we held our first worship service on March 16, 1997. We met in rented space in the oldest middle school in the city. Every Sunday, we hauled in the sound equipment and children's gear from trailers we kept in members' driveways.

I worked hard and long, seventy or eighty hours a week, with few days off, if any. That's what it takes to start something. It was my time to seize the opportunity to begin a new work. Today, more than a decade later, I look back at that time as a wonderful, special stage. For all its craziness, and for all my exhaustion, it was worth it. A church was born, and it continues strong to this day. It was appropriate to seize the opportunity before me. I was glad to be part of it.

The danger was that I would keep working at that pace and burn myself out. For a while after we were up and running, I tried to maintain an unsustainable pace—until some friends confronted me. I had to learn that, in a rhythmic approach to life, there are times to work like a madman and times to rest deeply.

Leroy is a good friend. I shared with him that starting a church is like having a baby. New parents don't appreciate those first years sufficiently. Only in looking back do we realize how precious that time was. My advice to him was to treasure the season of the start-up, to stop and celebrate, to pause and reflect on the wonderful blessings of starting a new enterprise. If I had it to do over again, I would embrace more of the blessings. I would stop to sense the joy, to realize the wonder of what we were creating.

In a rhythmic approach to life, there are times to work like a madman and times to rest deeply.

Too often, when we are starting a company, building a business, or raising kids, we are in such a rush that we don't take time to enjoy the blessings and the opportunities. We are consumed with doing the job and making life work. We miss the joy that could be ours if we would slow down and embrace the blessings of the season.

### OPENING OF THE SCHOOL YEAR

Beginnings provide unique opportunities. Last fall I gave the opening address to the faculty and staff of McKinney Christian Academy as they began the school year. Here is part of what I shared that morning:

> Today, I have one message for you: seize the start of school. You have a unique opportunity. Ask yourself, what time is it? And what opportunities does this time afford you? You are starting a season—it will be over in nine months—it has a rhythm to it.

In this season, God is giving you unique opportunities to seize. The opportunities are primarily people—students and staff. You can make a difference that may have an incredible impact in this world.

Beginnings are important. They set direction and tone for the year. You are to be part of the genesis of a new school year, classroom, and office. Seize the start. What can you do in the next few weeks that you cannot do later in the year? Right at the start, students and parents are asking: Am I going to like this teacher? How is this classroom going to be run?

**Set relationships:** You can never make a first impression twice.

**Set expectations:** Establish the standards and tone at the start.

**Set patterns:** Create healthy habits for yourself, students, and the staff.

The start of anything significant is an important season to seize. Beginnings set the direction that will determine the ending.

### AN EX-WIFE REQUESTS TO VISIT HER EX IN JAIL

Sometimes we must face very difficult realities. Though Maria had once hated her ex-husband, Geraldo, now that he had been sentenced to fifteen years in prison, she felt compassion for him. As a former police officer who had committed a sexual crime, he was facing the prospect of solitary confinement for a decade or more. Through the thick glass, Maria and Geraldo talked on the visiting room phones. He said he planned to just "fall asleep" like Rip van Winkle and wake up ten years later to do life better.

Even in very difficult seasons, you can look for unique

opportunities to seize. Maria asked Geraldo if he could think of unique opportunities that he could seize while in prison. He was blank. Of course, no one wants to be in prison, especially not in solitary confinement. But no matter what situation you are in, there are always opportunities to seize if you look hard enough.

> Even in very difficult seasons, you can look for unique opportunities to seize.

I will admit there are few blessings to embrace in prison. However, it was from prison that the apostle Paul wrote his most joyous letter, Philippians. And it is in that letter that he says he had learned to be content no matter what the circumstances. Even in prison, there are blessings to embrace.

Though few people would choose to spend ten years alone, what opportunities might such a time of isolation and solitude afford? How many times could Geraldo read through the Bible in ten years? How much of it could he memorize? This might be a time to grow close to God and study his Word in a way that will never come again. When Maria made this suggestion, Geraldo brightened at the idea and determined to find a Bible and get started. Even in prison, there are opportunities to seize.

While personal seasons provide bursts of opportunity, life stages offer extended opportunities to seize. During a season of years, we can find unique blessings to embrace that are only available during that stage.

## Seize Opportunities in Life Stages

Mike Jones is so stressed by trying to keep every ball in the air that he can hardly seize any opportunity. It's hard to grab a ball when you are already juggling more than you can handle. And yet Mike has awesome opportunities right before him. His kids want to spend time with him—that won't last forever. This is Mike's time to invest in his daughter's life on the soccer field and in his son's life at the Boy Scout campout. Winning "best yard" or serving on the board of the local food pantry can wait. Now is the time for Mike to seize the opportunity with his kids.

This doesn't mean he won't have to occasionally bail out for a crisis at work (such as the phone call he received that Saturday about being needed at work), but he should release the expectation that he will leave the campout early to go see his parents. If Mike would slow down long enough to count how few years he has left with his children at this stage, he would be more intentional about seizing the moments.

### MY DAD'S ART

My dad, who is now in his midseventies, is seizing the opportunity to paint. While I was growing up, my dad worked hard at his dental practice and didn't have much time for painting. But he always enjoyed art. When he was working as a dentist, he could have been resentful about not having time to paint. But he wasn't. He was seizing the opportunities of his current season to build a dental practice and develop a financial base for his later years. Now that he's retired from dentistry, he could resent the fact that he no longer has the physical stamina to work on his feet all day; but he doesn't. He appreciates the years he had to work, and now he focuses on the joy of painting watercolors.

In this new stage of life, he can take multiple art courses and spend hours and hours painting. What an opportunity! He is studying how to draw human faces and sculpt hands. A few months ago, he was able to go to a weeklong seminar with a visiting art professor.

How fulfilling for my dad to do what he has always appreciated but never had time to develop. Tamara and I have in our master bedroom a beautiful painting that my dad created of a country church. People offer to buy his work. He has considered putting his paintings for sale online and showing some in a gallery. This never would have happened, and should not have happened, in earlier life stages. But now is his time to paint, and he is making the most of it.

### SINGLE FREEDOM

When you are unattached, you have freedom to make plans on the spur of the moment and change them without consulting a partner. Embrace the freedom of singleness—the opportunities to spend your money and time as you please. Invest in what matters to you, in what makes a difference in your world. Experience the joy of service, volunteering for a cause that changes lives.

Embrace the freedom of singleness—the opportunities to spend your money and time as you please.

### FIRSTS

Live fully in your current rhythm. If you have a two-year-old, enjoy his or her blossoming personality. If you are in college, rejoice in your freedom rather than resenting your poverty. Enjoy your firsts. Embrace your first car, your first apartment. They are usually not the finest, but often they're the most cherished. Someday you may not remember all the places you have lived or the cars you have driven, but you usually remember the first ones. (My first car was a very used, red Ford Pinto.)

During times of high activity earlier in my life, I rarely slowed down to enjoy the blessings of those days. Starts are exhausting and wonderful, whether it is a new baby, a new home, or a new church. When you are at the beginning, it doesn't feel like a time to slow down; it doesn't even seem possible. But you can choose to rejoice in the start.

When you have kids, their stages make a big impact on your life stages. It is the stages of their lives that offer you wonderful opportunities to seize and enjoy, if you will use rhythm strategy. The cliché is true: they really do grow up fast. The preschool phase of raising kids feels like an eternity when you are in it, but it is so brief in the span of life. So are the teenage years—seven years per child. That's it. Seize the opportunities that are unique to each stage, and enjoy their distinct blessings.

Seize the opportunities that are unique to each stage, and enjoy their distinct blessings.

Last year I was soaking up every moment I had left with my daughter, who was a senior in high school. And then my youngest, Ben, turned sixteen and got his first car, a 4x4 1987 Blazer. My kids are almost gone. I can feel this stage coming to a close, so I'm determined to seize every opportunity to enjoy this season with my wife and my kids.

## GOOD-NIGHT KISSES

Parents of younger children feel chained to bedtime. Little ones want Mommy or Daddy to tuck them into bed. At my current stage of life, I would give my right arm to have those days back. At that time in my kids' lives, I was working two jobs and going to graduate school. If I was home for bedtime at all, I was exhausted and often just wanted to get it over with. But what an opportunity I missed.

Embrace the blessing of your children's kisses and hugs. If they want to do a jiggly dance, dance with all your heart. Drink deeply of the longing looks they give you with their big eyes looking up from the pillow. When they ask again and again for one more kiss good night, keep kissing them over and over, as much for yourself as for them.

There are only a few years between infancy and adolescence when kids want Daddy or Mommy to read a story, pray with them, tuck them into bed, and stay with them until they fall asleep. Those are precious moments. What an opportunity to invest in their young lives.

### TAXI TIME

Parents of school-age kids often complain about being a taxi service. You spend your time and gas money driving kids to school and back, then to lessons and practices and friends' homes. It feels as if you spend your entire life in the car. But rather than resenting the taxi-service years, can you see the latent opportunity? Your children are captive with you for the length of the commute. Talk. Drop the headphones connected to the DVD player, video game, or iPod. Instead, seize the opportunity for relationship, for building into their lives. About the time they turn sixteen and can drive, those taxi days will be gone, and you will not have as much one-on-one time to spend with them.

My children tell tales—they're getting to be tall tales now—of how I used to give them Bible trivia drills on the way to school. I tried to make it fun, and we laughed a lot, and they learned. Now, of course, as they tell the story, it sounds like I was a crazy person forcing them to memorize arcane facts; but we all smile remembering those drives to school.

Celebrate the blessings of youth, the excitement and energy of the teenage years.

### ICE-CREAM CONES

Celebrate the blessings of youth, the excitement and energy of the teenage years. Schools give out awards and have ceremonies all year long. Take part. Seize the moment. Be there for your sons or daughters. Run the video camera and celebrate their parts in the school play, the musical, the band, the volleyball team, the debate competition, whatever it is. Experience the joy with them. We started an ice-cream tradition in the Miller household. Almost any event was a good enough excuse to go to Braum's for an ice-cream cone.

### HIGH SCHOOL FOOTBALL

In the teen years, you have the chance to enjoy high school football again. In Texas, football is king. The "Friday night lights" come on and the town comes out to cheer on the good guys. At halftime, the band plays its show and the drill team dances its routine. Moms and dads volunteer to serve concessions and take tickets. You may hate football, but here is a brief window of time, a short season, to be with your kids and enter their world.

### COLLEGE LIFE

I rushed through college in a hurry to grow up. I graduated in three years. Why? I wanted to get on to the next thing—and to save money—but I wish I had lingered in that stage to relish university life. I wish I had taken the full four or five years that most people take and had experienced all that was available in that stage, which is now gone forever. Given the chance to do it again, I would embrace more of the awesome benefits that college life has to offer. I would go to more sports games, visit more museums, and go to more concerts. I would play intramurals and take bowling classes in the student center. But we do not get to relive most stages of our lives. We get one shot. When we live our lives in rhythm, we make the most of every season and stage of life.

### EMPTY NEST

My wife and I are on the verge of the empty nest. We are telling ourselves to welcome the blessings that this next season will bring. It is tempting to miss the kids who have already left home, and we do. We feel the increased silence in the home. It's uncomfortable, but we see the blessings, too. We're beginning to taste the joy of being at home alone together. We can share quiet dinners. We can finally talk at length without being interrupted fifty times. We are beginning to go to the gym together in the evenings, seizing the new opportunity to work out more than we ever did when all our kids were at home. Our joy grows as we choose to enjoy the benefits of the empty nest.

> We do not get to relive most stages of our lives. We get one shot. When we live our lives in rhythm, we make the most of every season and stage of life.

When your kids are grown, you have new freedom—a freedom that gives you fresh opportunities to serve the world. You have more time and often more money than at any other point in your life. And yet I see many empty nesters squandering their time and money on themselves. Jesus said he did not come to be served but to serve. Consider the huge opportunities that God has afforded you at this stage of your life. During this season, you have so much that you can give back in service and leadership.

### ENJOYING THE LATTER STAGES OF LIFE

My mom is in her seventies. After reading an early version of this book, she wrote to me, saying, "I don't know how many more years we will have together, so I want to spend more time enjoying your dad. We have both been hard-charging all our lives. Frankly, I am having a difficult time realizing that I can't accomplish as much as I used to. Reading this book is helping me accept this season of life, to relax and enjoy common, everyday pleasures such as sitting on the patio with your dad, watching the birds, squirrels, and rabbits."

Ray and Anne Ortlund—best-selling authors, radio speakers, retreat leaders and mentors—have influenced the lives of countless people. In a magazine article, the interviewer asked Anne, "As you look back, what have you learned about finishing well?"

Anne replied, "We asked ourselves, 'What can we do now that we couldn't do earlier?' We've discovered that pastors half our age who are hurting—and most of them are—won't tell their peers or district superintendents, but they will tell someone who's old. They'll pour their hearts out. . . . They come to our home and stay in a hotel overnight. From nine to five, we talk about where they're headed, where they've come from, their marriage, time management—whatever they want to talk about."[1]

Retirement takes your freedom to a whole new level.

Since this article was published, Ray has left this world, but in his last years, though he could no longer travel, he and Anne seized the opportunity to mentor young church leaders.

Retirement takes your freedom to a whole new level. If you have health and time, use them to carry out your life's mission in wonderful ways that were not open to you in previous stages when you had to work full-time.

When you move to a new place, you have the opportunity for a fresh start. When you have lived in a place a long time, you have the opportunity for rich, deep relationships that span years. In both cases, there are latent opportunities to fulfill your life's mission, if you will be alert to look for them.

Exchange burnout for fulfillment by releasing false expectations and seizing unique opportunities in this season and stage of your life. In this way, you will find a better life. A wise person slows down to savor a little baby's breath, to linger over a friend's embrace, to celebrate a victory won. While the ideas are fresh in your mind, take a moment to consider opportunities you could seize right now in your personal seasons and life stage.

---

LIFE EXERCISE: *Make a list, beginning with the following phrase: "I will seize these unique opportunities in this kairos season . . ."*

# 8
# Kairos Strategy #3: Anticipate What's Next

*May the God of hope fill you with all joy and peace as you trust in him, so that you may overflow with hope by the power of the Holy Spirit.*

ROMANS 15:13

Anticipation breeds hope. When you feel stuck in your current stage, know that it will not last forever; the next stage is on the horizon. Nothing stays the same.

If you feel you cannot stand to change one more diaper, know that in a few years you will be done. If your teenagers are wearing you out, it won't be long before they enter adulthood. If you are sick of college, look ahead; you will walk across the stage, turn your tassel, and then homework and exams will be behind you. If you cannot stand to serve one more customer at the register, realize you will likely not work there forever. All our life stages are comparatively brief in light of the entire scope of our lives. Most stages are just long enough to fully embrace them before we see them in the rearview mirror. So even if you're in a season now that feels as if it will never end, take heart. The next stage is just over the horizon. Though we should certainly live fully in the present season of our lives, looking ahead to what's next can give us hope.

Despair comes from feeling stuck. When it feels as if you will always be nothing but a taxi service, driving kids from one activity to another, it's easy to allow negative emotions to cloud your vision. If we're not careful, our emotions can spiral downward, taking us lower and lower into depression. The more we consider the difficulty of our current jobs, finances, or relationships, the more we might despair. When we're in the middle of the tunnel of chaos, we cannot see the light at the end of the tunnel—but it's there.

Hope and anticipation turn on the light. If you can see the opening at the end of the tunnel, you have the ability to keep crawling, knowing you are close to getting out. Even though you are still in the tunnel, moving toward the light with hope inspires you to continue with new strength. Just ahead there is a new start, a new stage, a new season, whether it means a new job, a new city, or new relationships.

When we're in the middle of the tunnel of chaos, we cannot see the light at the end of the tunnel—but it's there.

Our English word *hope* can be pretty weak. We often use it to describe something that might happen but probably won't. We talk about "hoping against hope." For instance, when you get an envelope in the mail from Publisher's Clearinghouse that says, "You may already have won a million dollars," you think, *I hope I have*—but you know you probably haven't. Every day, millions of people buy a lottery ticket hoping to win the big drawing for millions of dollars, but the odds against winning are tremendous.

In contrast to our English word for hope is the concept behind the Greek word *elpis*, which describes a sure, absolute confidence that something is going to happen. For instance, hope (*elpis*) is the confident, joyful expectation of the completion of God's grace in Jesus Christ. The biblical concept of hope means something you can count on with utter and complete confidence. You may or may not stay in your current home; you may or may not keep your job; but one thing you can absolutely count on: heaven is real. You can stake your life on that. Biblical hope is an anchor for our souls.

The kairos rhythm strategy of anticipating what's next is built on a kind of hope that is closer to the biblical *elpis* than to the English *hope*. When you anticipate what's coming ahead, that expectation fuels the hope that gives you a better life.

### THE WEDDING IS ON THE CALENDAR

I thought being engaged was supposed to be a fun, magical time. It was not. Tamara and I felt as if we were sort of married, in that we were committed and I had given her a ring, but we weren't married. We were still living in separate places.

> When you anticipate what's coming ahead, that expectation fuels the hope that gives you a better life.

Because we were young, the in-law problems were pretty intense. Her parents wanted to hold on to her as a daughter, and my parents wanted to hold on to me as a son; yet they were all trying to let go. At the same time, we were trying to plan a wedding, in which even the choice of songs threatened to become a life-and-death matter.

In the midst of the tension over how many guests *not* to invite, Tamara and I kept telling each other, "In three months, we're going to be married. It doesn't matter—we can hold on." "We can hang in there because in *two* months we are going to be married." "In twenty-seven days and twelve hours we are going to be married. So we are going to get through this." We were able to hang in there and weather the storm of preparations because the wedding was coming. Anticipation. Hope.

## HE'S COMING HOME!

Recently, I read a request from a young wife asking me to pray for her because her husband is being deployed to Iraq for nine months. How is she going to get through this next season? How will she avoid despair on cold nights and rainy days when the heater breaks and she is pulling her hair out because of the kids? She is going to look forward with incredible anticipation to the day her husband will return. She will count down the days, telling herself, *He'll be home soon.*

When she gets the letter saying, "I'm on my way," she will tape it on the refrigerator door and read it several times every day. It'll be tough at the house by herself; she'll be working hard, and she'll be lonely and worried for her husband. But with hope and anticipation, she'll be able to say to herself, *Thirty-seven more days, and he will be home—he'll be home! And we will be together, and everything will be okay!* Hope is life sustaining.

Of course, our hopes do not always materialize. Sometimes the wedding is called off or the soldier doesn't make it home. When a crisis comes, a new rhythm begins; you have an unexpectedly huge wave to ride. The three kairos rhythm strategies will help you ride the new wave well.

In times of crisis, the same strategies apply. After taking time to grieve well, look for expectations to release, as difficult as that may be. Release the expectation that you'll get back together, the expectation that he'll walk through that door any minute. Identify, seize, and embrace unique opportunities in this challenging and trying season. Find new hope in anticipating what's next, because this overwhelming wave will not last. It, too, will pass, and a new day will come.

> Anticipation can be short- or long-term. Anticipate both the next season to come and your next life stage.

Anticipation can be short- or long-term. Anticipate both the next season(s) to come and your next life stage.

## Anticipate Coming Personal Seasons

What is about to end in your life? What is about to begin? Kairos seasons are not as fully predictable as chronos cycles.

Winter comes every year, but a new job does not. However, some seasons can be planned and should be planned. Think about your energy rhythmically. After an intense season, you need time to recover, time to build up reserves so you can move into another intense season full of strength and energy. Sometimes you can see a high-stress time coming and anticipate it.

### CAPITAL CAMPAIGN

As I have experimented with living rhythmically, I have found that in a season of hard work, it makes sense to plan a time of rest on the other side. When we needed to build a larger building because our church was growing, it meant we had to raise money. Raising millions of dollars takes tremendous effort spiritually, emotionally, and physically. Looking at the task ahead, I knew that for about three months I was going to work like crazy, attending dozens of meetings, speaking to groups, meeting with individual donors, designing communication pieces, working with the architect, and more.

The power of expectation gives the endurance it takes to keep working hard.

To help myself and my family live through this intense time, I scheduled a week's vacation after it was all over. My whole family looked forward to that week. They knew that Dad was going to work like crazy for about three months, but then we were going to take a week off to just enjoy one another and relax. The vacation was on the calendar. They could anticipate it.

The power of expectation gives the endurance it takes to keep working hard. When you know that right around the corner is a rest, a break, a vacation, you can keep going full-out on the task at hand. Plan times of rest and renewal after an intense time of work to give yourself something to hope for during the long, tough days.

### FINAL EXAMS AND HOLIDAY BREAKS

School works in a rhythmic way: after final exams comes winter or summer break. If you are in school, you can look ahead and anticipate the short season of final exams. Think rhythmically. Finals should be a season of late-night studying and hard work. You intentionally push yourself to study for days on end, but you anticipate that Christmas break or summer vacation is just around the corner. The semester is almost over. Anticipating the break fills you with hope to persevere in the library.

### ON THE ROAD

If you know you have a season of frequent travel or long work hours ahead during which you will be away from loved ones, take some time off work just before and just after. This is not balance—trying to keep everything even; this is rhythm—taking advantage of the natural ebbs and flows to keep you fully engaged in every area of your life. When you are traveling, fully engage in your business. When you come home from a business trip, fully embrace your family.

### TRAGEDY

Though you know when to expect final exams, many seasons happen with no warning. Sometimes a loved one dies suddenly. Whether you are rested or not, it is time to expend tremendous emotional energy. If you are the closest relative, you will be making funeral arrangements and taking care of hundreds of details.

For a season, you will be intensely engaged in closing out

a life, in grieving a loss. Knowing you will exhaust yourself in grief, plan a time of rest. Ask for time off a few months after the funeral. You will be drained. You will need renewal. During the time you are consumed with the aftermath of your loved one's death, the expectation of time for recovery and renewal can fuel you with hope.

### PLAN YOUR REST DURING YOUR WORK

Increase your anticipation by planning the downtime during the time of exertion. Figuring out where you will go and what you will do puts your mind into that place. You can smell the pine trees. You can feel the ocean waves rolling over your toes. You can feel the wind in your face as you ride down the winding road. Look ahead to where you will be, and imagine being there.

> Increase your anticipation by planning the downtime during the time of exertion.

Right now, my wife and I are planning a special trip to celebrate our twenty-fifth wedding anniversary. We're going to Isla Mujeres off the coast of Cancún on the Yucatán Peninsula in Mexico. Hours of anticipation have been invested checking out hotels to find the best one, looking at excursions such as swimming with dolphins, and checking out Mayan ruins. Now the flights are booked and the hotel room is reserved. Six months from the time I write this, we will be sitting on our balcony overlooking the beautiful Caribbean Sea.

### FINANCIAL WAVES

Some financial peaks and valleys can be anticipated. Financial advisers have well-developed analyses of a person's typical earning and spending cycles over a lifetime. A wise adviser can help you anticipate the financial waves you will ride over the next several years. In a season with young children, you need more life insurance; as you get closer to retirement, you need more investments. In one stage, you may buy a house; in another stage, ideally, it is paid for. Education, weddings, children, and retirement all come in waves. Anticipation can give you hope to ride the next financial wave well because you have seen it coming and have planned for it.

### SABBATICALS

After a long stretch of high stress, you need a long break. About four years after the start of our church, I was deeply tired. The elders, the governing board of the church, granted me a six-week sabbatical in the summer of 2001. I needed it. That deep rest overcame my bone-tiredness. The tiredness itself was not bad; it's healthy to work hard, so hard that you are exhausted. What's foolish is to never stop and renew your energy. A rhythmic approach to life encourages seasons of high intensity that require personal sacrifice, but these times should be followed by a season of rest and renewal.

> It's healthy to work hard, so hard that you are exhausted. What's foolish is to never stop and renew your energy.

Whether or not our employers will grant a sabbatical, most of us will need to take a long rest at some point in our lives. We need to stop for our own health. If we don't, we run the risk of our bodies stopping us involuntarily with a physical illness or an emotional breakdown. You can avoid that kind of collapse by choosing to take a sabbatical periodically.

## Anticipate Your Next Life Stage

Though not all kairos rhythms can be predicted (who knows when a windfall or a crisis may come?), life stages can be anticipated. We know we will age and experience predictable changes. It's the same with children. Their stages can be anticipated: terrible twos, noisy nines, preteen issues, puberty, and high school excitement. Each child is different, but you can prepare for what is likely to occur.

On the other hand, no one knows what tomorrow holds, so we cannot presume on the future. Rarely does everything go as planned. Along the way, children veer off the desired course, couples separate and divorce, jobs are lost. But even though we don't know with certainty what will happen in the future, we can anticipate that (if we live long enough) we will likely bury our parents, face physical limitations, and (if we have children) see our grandchildren.

If you really don't like the stage of life you're in right now, use the power of anticipation to give yourself hope.

If you really don't like the stage of life you're in right now, use the power of anticipation to give yourself hope. Your current stage will not last forever. There is another stage coming.

## WHAT DO YOU DO WITH A BABY?

Some people love the early stages of a child's life. Most everyone thinks infants are cute. But I did not know what to do with my eldest son when he was first born. My wife was a natural, but I could never figure out why the kid was crying; I just begged him to be quiet.

Once he could carry on a conversation and toss a ball, I did better. After my first child, of course, I knew what was coming with the others, and I could tell myself, "Pretty soon this baby is going to walk and talk, and we will have great times together." Anticipating the days to come empowered me in the days when I felt helpless and frustrated.

### SENIORITIS

Often toward the end of one stage, we get restless for something new. We are sick of the stage we're in. In the spring of their final year of high school, most students contract the classic disease "senioritis." They are done with high school before it is over. They have already been accepted to a college or have a job lined up, so why keep going to class? Other than graduation, there isn't much left. In their minds, they are too mature for high school now—they're done and they want out.

We experience senioritis to one degree or another near the end of each life stage; it is just more obvious in high school. For example, many parents are also ready for their last child to leave home. However, we must avoid the temptation to let go of our parenting responsibilities too soon.

### TRANSITIONS

When you know your job will soon be over, it's hard to finish well. Whether you are leaving for another company, being laid off, or retiring, you are done emotionally before you pull out of the parking lot for the last time. Once you see the end coming, you start ending it in your heart. If you do that too soon, your last months will be hard and feel like forever.

> Stress comes from trying to surf a wave before it arrives. . . . You can't ride the wave until it touches your board.

Use the power of anticipation as motivation to finish well. You know a new stage is coming. Let the expectation of the new season give you hope today to work hard as you complete your current responsibilities in your present rhythm. Stress comes from trying to surf a wave before it arrives. That is frustrating and unproductive. You can't ride the wave until it touches your board.

What is the next stage you are about to enter? For me, it is the empty-nest stage. How can I prepare myself so that I'm not caught off guard? What can I look forward to expectantly that will give me hope today? I am anticipating more time with Tamara. I am anticipating a quieter, cleaner, more orderly home.

What seasons do you see coming in the near future? Fill your life with hope through anticipation.

**Living in Time with Your Kairos Rhythms**

*Release false expectations* that don't fit your kairos rhythms.

*Seize unique opportunities* afforded by your kairos rhythms.

*Anticipate* the next kairos rhythms just ahead of you.

*Experience the power* of trust, focus, expectation.

*Reap the benefits* of peace, fulfillment, and hope.

Rhythms are not to be resisted, managed, or ignored; they're to be embraced. Just as in surfing, we make the best use of life transitions when we anticipate the breaks and bring our lives into alignment with the natural rhythm and direction of the waves. To live in time with our kairos rhythms, we employ the three kairos strategies: release expectations, seize opportunities, and anticipate what's next.

Think about vacations. When you're single, you're free to take whatever kind of wild, exotic vacations you want: thrill-seeking adventures in the mountains and on the beaches. You can meet all kinds of interesting people and stay up late at night talking with them. But you can wreck your joy by resenting the fact that you don't have a partner with whom to share the experience.

If you will release false expectations that do not fit your current kairos rhythms, you will find peace. This may not be your time for a romantic getaway; maybe this is your time for the kids. If you will seize the opportunity to make memories with your kids—carrying out your mission to be a great parent—you will find fulfillment. If you will embrace the blessing of holding your child's hand as you jump the little waves at the beach or walk through the amusement park or hike the beginners trail, you will find joy. If you anticipate the future day when you will hold your spouse's hand as you walk the beach alone together at sunset, you will find hope.

The key to maximizing your kairos rhythms is to know what "time" it is in your life, and to learn how to live in time with your life's rhythms. In the next part, we will look at how to find more peace, fulfillment, and hope in your chronos rhythms by employing the three chronos rhythm strategies: pacing yourself, building rituals, and oscillating between work and rest.

---

LIFE EXERCISE: *Make a list, beginning with the following phrase: "I can anticipate the following personal seasons and life stages coming . . ."*

*How will you prepare to release expectations and seize unique opportunities in the coming seasons?*

PART III

# Chronos Rhythm Strategies

# 9
# The Five Chronos Cycles

> *The sun rises and the sun sets, and hurries back to where it rises.*
>
> ECCLESIASTES 1:5

Light and dark. Day and night. The moon waxes and wanes. Seasons alternate from winter to spring, summer to fall. We live in a large ecosystem that moves rhythmically in seasons, tides, currents, and cycles. We can fight them or follow them.

When we try to live as if natural cycles did not exist, as if all time progressed in a uniform, linear fashion, we frustrate ourselves and increase our stress. Some of our burnout comes from not recognizing nature's rhythms and living in harmony with them. When enough plates crash to the floor, despair takes us down.

Over the past twenty years, other authors have written on effective time management with increasing sophistication. In *First Things First*, Stephen Covey presents his model as the fourth generation of time management.[1] *Your Life in Rhythm* offers a fifth-generation model, a move beyond time management.

How can you move beyond time management? By shifting your mental model from "management" to "flow." You cannot manage time. Time happens, and time is the same for everyone. By growing in your understanding of how time flows, you can flow *with* it more harmoniously and effectively. Shift the focus of your attention from *time* to *yourself*.

Though we do need to better understand the flow of time, that insight will still not allow us to alter time or to manage it. Our focus must shift from managing time to allowing our lives to flow in harmony with time's cycles.

## The Movement of Time

In chapter 4, we discussed the differences between two kinds of rhythm: kairos and chronos. Kairos rhythms are experienced, lived times, which happen in unpredictable patterns. To flow well with them, we employ the strategies of releasing expectations, seizing opportunities, and anticipating what's next. Chronos rhythms are *measured times*, which happen in predicable patterns. Clocks and calendars keep chronos time.

Our focus must shift from managing time to allowing our lives to flow in harmony with time's cycles.

Life is not merely a succession of uniform segments of time called seconds, minutes, and hours. A rhythmic approach resists the mechanizing and commoditizing of time. Time flows in what I am calling chronos cycles. Chronos cycles are not some new invention; they're not the latest artificial time-management system to impose on our lives. These cycles are the way life happens on earth for all organisms, including human beings.

Most every language has words to describe these cyclical

frequencies. These cycles are not mysterious or new; they have always formed the temporal fabric of life. Though cultures have created unique calendars, these regularly repeating chronos cycles are not a cultural artifice of one civilization or another. They were not invented. Rather, the five chronos cycles are rooted in the created order.[2]

We have commoditized time—imagining that we can save it, spend it, or be out of it. Contrary to Benjamin Franklin's perspective, time is not money. Franklin equated time to money in his influential *Autobiography* and in *Poor Richard's Almanac*.[3] He reduced time to a unit of exchange. But we are not in control of time, nor can we exchange it. No one has more or has less of it. We have commercialized time, falsely imagining that because we can measure it more precisely, we can then manage it more fully, that we can control it because we mark it, count it, and watch it. This is an illusion.

Time is neither a commodity nor a mechanized unit—it is the flow of our lives in this universe, with our specific configuration of sun, moon, and planets in their relative rotations and orbits. We did not invent time, only ways to observe its passing. Imagining ourselves in "control" of time leads us falsely into a balance model, in which we attempt to equalize or proportion the units of time we spend on each area of our lives. But there is a better way to live.

Imagining ourselves in "control" of time leads us falsely into a balance model.

City dwellers may have a harder time grasping the cycles than those who live closer to the land. The cycles are simple, natural, and basic. You do not need charts, or even words, to embrace the five chronos cycles. If you are alive, you experience them.

Humans have lived in these cycles for thousands of years

in all different cultures, climates, and civilizations. They are intuitive for Bushmen in Africa, Native Americans on the western plains of North America, hunters in the jungle, and farmers in China, who have all followed these cycles for millennia.

When we study music, we first learn basic time signatures. Later, we discover variations of many kinds, but first we need to learn the fundamentals. So it is with life; there are many rhythms and variations, but as a beginning, we must learn how to live in the five basic environmental chronos cycles:

**Orbital (annual):** based on the earth orbiting the sun, about every 365 days
**Seasonal (quarterly):** based on the tilt of the earth shifting, about every 90 days
**Lunar (monthly):** based on the cycle of the moon, about every 29.5 days
**Sabbath (weekly):** based on the creation pattern of seven days
**Rotational (daily):** based on the rotation of the earth, about every 24 hours

In this part of the book, we will learn how to live intentionally in harmony with the orbital, seasonal, lunar, sabbatical, and rotational rhythms that are built into the created order. We will explore three chronos rhythm strategies: pace yourself, build rituals, and oscillate between work and rest. Applying these strategies will increase your peace, fulfillment, and hope.

Busyness is exacerbated when we attempt to live in the same way day after day, year after year, without paying attention to cycles that structure our existence. Unneeded guilt comes from the insane attempt to keep a constant, uniform pace. Applying these rhythm strategies in the five chronos cycles will free us from the ridiculous busyness treadmill that drives us crazy. You can find the ancient, foundational cycles in the Bible.

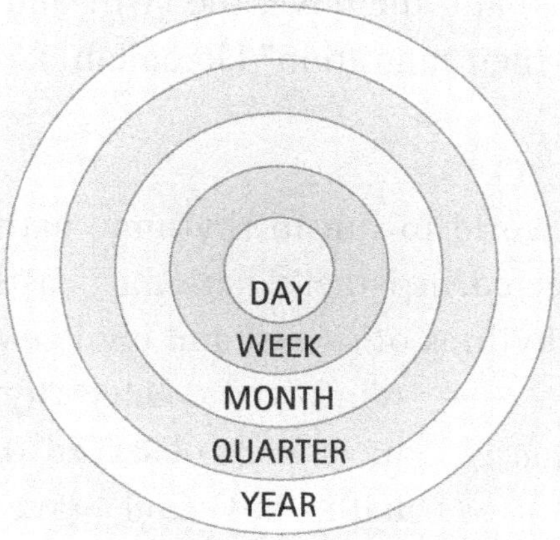


## GOD'S CREATION OF THE RHYTHMIC WORLD

God created the world to function rhythmically. Even the description of Creation in Genesis 1 uses a rhythmic, Hebrew narrative form. Each day follows a pattern, ending with the phrase "and God saw that it was good."

God created seasons, days, and years. "And God said, 'Let there be lights in the expanse of the sky to separate the day from the night, and let them serve as signs to mark seasons and days and years'" (Genesis 1:14).

After the Flood, God promised that these patterns will continue. "As long as the earth endures, seedtime and harvest, cold and heat, summer and winter, day and night will never cease" (Genesis 8:22).

The psalmist declares, "The moon marks off the seasons, and the sun knows when to go down" (Psalm 104:19); and the prophet Jeremiah affirms, "Even the stork in the sky knows her appointed seasons, and the dove, the swift and the thrush observe the time of their migration" (Jeremiah 8:7).

## ISRAEL'S FEAST CYCLES

God created the world to run in rhythmic patterns, and these patterns are reflected in Israel's national feasts. God directed Israel to follow rhythms of sacred and civil celebration, which reinforced created rhythms. The Jews have long observed the weekly Sabbath, but God gave several other rhythms as well.

God created the world to run in rhythmic patterns.

Every year, Israel celebrated an annual rhythm of festivals and sacrifices, including the holy Day of Atonement (see Exodus 30:10) and three annual feasts—the Feast of Unleavened Bread, the Feast of Weeks, and the Feast of Tabernacles (see 2 Chronicles 8:13). The longest rhythm was the Jubilee. Every fifty years, Israel was to carry out a year of liberty, in which everyone (including indentured servants) and all property were to be returned to their original state (see Leviticus 25:10-13).

As God instructed, each year Israel was to make offerings tied to the movement of the moon. "With each bull [sacrificed] there is to be a drink offering of half a hin of wine; with the ram, a third of a hin; and with each lamb, a quarter of a hin. This is the monthly burnt offering to be made at each new moon during the year" (Numbers 28:14).

Annual and lunar cycles were complemented by the weekly Sabbath rest, based on the pattern of God's creation. "For in six days the LORD made the heavens and the earth, the sea, and all that is in them, but he rested on the seventh day. Therefore the LORD blessed the Sabbath day and made it holy" (Exodus 20:11).

In Exodus 34:21, God gave Israel a weekly rhythmic rest: "Six days you shall labor, but on the seventh day you shall rest; even during the plowing season and harvest you must rest." Even the Jubilee was part of a cycle of years based on the Sabbath. "Count off seven sabbaths of years—seven times seven years—so that the seven sabbaths of years amount to a period of forty-nine years. Then . . . consecrate the fiftieth year and proclaim liberty throughout the land to all its inhabitants" (Leviticus 25:8-10).

In addition to the Jubilee, annual, lunar, and Sabbath rhythms, Israel also carried out daily offerings and times of prayer. "These are in addition to the monthly and daily burnt offerings with their grain offerings and drink offerings as specified. They are offerings made to the LORD by fire—a pleasing aroma" (Numbers 29:6). The Hebrews model a rhythmic life according to divinely inspired patterns. These spiritual rhythms correspond to natural rhythms formed in the created order. Only recently has science begun to discover the deep resonances of this rhythmic order.

Spiritual rhythms correspond to natural rhythms formed in the created order.

## CHRONOBIOLOGY—AN EMERGING FRONTIER

Chronobiology, a relatively new field, is revealing a new frontier of natural rhythms. It is the study (*logos*) of life's (*bios*) structure in time (*chronos*). Franz Halberg, the founder of modern chronobiology, began his experiments in the 1940s and headed the chronobiology laboratories at the University of Minnesota.[4]

*Rhythms of Life: The Biological Clocks That Control the Daily Lives of Every Living Thing*, by Russell Foster and Leon Kreitzman, brings the insights of chronobiology to the general public. The authors describe how biological clocks allow organisms to adapt and respond to the rhythms that result from the movement of the Earth. "Biological clocks impose a structure that enables organisms to change their behavioral priorities in relation to the time of day, month, or year."[5]

According to Foster and Kreitzman, "Today there are probably well over a thousand scientists working on the basic science of biological time. At least ten times as many are working on applying this information in medicine, agriculture, horticulture, manned space flights, and warfare."[6] A new subdiscipline, chronotherapy, has discovered that *when* you take medicines influences how they affect you.

When we try to impose unnatural structure that is out of harmony with created rhythms, we generate "noise."

When we try to impose unnatural structure that is out of harmony with created rhythms, we generate "noise." "All of us in the developed world now live in a '24/7' society," write Foster and Kreitzman. "This imposed structure is in conflict with our basic biology. The impact can be seen in our struggle to balance our daily lives with the stresses this places on our physical health and mental well-being. We are now aware of this fundamental tension between the way we want to live and the way we are built to live. It is hoped that our developing understanding of the basic biology will provide us with a means to resolve this fundamental dilemma of modern living."[7]

I strongly concur with Foster and Kreitzman's analysis, which correctly identifies our impossible struggle against our basic biological timing and environmental rhythms. No wonder we feel so much stress. Shifting our paradigm from balance to rhythm will help resolve this fundamental tension. Rather than seeking to balance our lives, we should seek to live in time with nature's rhythms. As scientists are discovering, that aim will lead to healthier lives.

My concern is how to apply the insights of chronobiology to our daily lives. How can we live better lives by paying attention to our biological clocks, which are in harmony with the natural cycles?

## The Five Chronos Cycles

The five chronos cycles are determined by the shape and movement of our solar system. Many people grasp life's chronos cycles intuitively; women tend to be especially good at this. You may or may not have this ability. My hope is to enhance your intuitive insights.

### ANNUAL (ORBITAL) RHYTHMS

The orbit of the Earth around the sun results in a period that is 365 days, 6 hours, 9 minutes, and 10 seconds long. Even the slightest shift in this orbital pattern would end all life on Earth. If we were a bit closer to the sun, we would burn up; a little farther away, and we would freeze; a greater tilt in our axis would throw off the gravitational pull.[8] This orbital pattern holds true in every culture and has been true in every century of human existence.

> Though we understand the concept of a year, few of us plan annually. And yet every year brings the same cycle.

Though we understand the concept of a year, few of us plan annually. And yet every year brings the same cycle. If you are a mom of school-age kids, you know the school year in your bones. You can sense when it is time for open house, report cards, or spring break. New Year's Day is the only holiday celebrated in most countries of the world.

Wherever you live, your climate follows a yearly cycle that affects all other annual cycles. Most of us swim in the summer, not the winter, and we trade hot coffee for frozen coffee drinks. Physically, seasons bring changes for our bodies, whether that is fresh energy from the warmth of the sun or seasonal depression for those far from the equator enduring days of limited daylight. Allergy and arthritis sufferers are keenly aware of seasonal changes.

Since at least the time of Hippocrates, scholars have been intrigued by seasonal influences on human experiences. Researchers in biometeorology have noted, for instance, that death rates in northern cultures peak during the winter; marriages peak in June, and births in late summer; winter leads to relatively high rates of depression; romantic relationships between college students tend to break up during the months of May, June, September, December, and January.

### QUARTERLY (SEASONAL) RHYTHMS

Each year contains four seasons. Though the seasons may be more pronounced and spectacular in New England than in Texas, all the world experiences changes based on the elliptical orbit of the Earth in relation to the sun. The natural basis for seasonal rhythms is not weather but the movement of the Earth in relation to the sun. Temperature changes are heavily latitude dependent, and the seasons reverse in the Southern and Northern hemispheres. No matter where you live on Earth, you experience the four seasons because their basis is astronomical.

The Earth's rotational axis is tilted at an angle of 23.44 degrees in relation to the orbital plane, and this tilt causes the seasons as the North and South poles lean toward or away from the sun. As a consequence, for half a year (from around March 20, the vernal equinox, to September 23, the autumnal equinox), the Northern Hemisphere tips toward the sun, with the maximum tilt around June 21, which is the summer solstice and the longest day of the year. For the other half of the year, the Southern Hemisphere has this honor, with the maximum tilt around December 21, the winter solstice.[9] The seasons have important implications for organisms. For instance, seasons dictate when animals can breed and when some must enter hibernation.

Planting time is followed by cultivating, harvesting, and a resting or fallow time.

Agricultural communities understand the seasons more richly than do city dwellers. Planting time is followed by cultivating, harvesting, and a resting or fallow time, not because farmers arbitrarily made up those times but because nature presents them in seasonal cycles.

Most of us overestimate what we can accomplish in a day or a week, but we underestimate what we can accomplish in a season. Many of us can sustain our focus for a week, but most of us lose focus over the course of three months. Developing a seasonal pace can help us live more healthy and productive lives. Although businesses often plan based on quarters (four three-month cycles per year), we seldom do in our personal lives. But by envisioning what we want to accomplish over a quarter of the year, we can take some large steps toward carrying out our life's mission.

## MONTHLY (LUNAR) RHYTHMS

The orbital characteristics of the moon generate the lunar month (29.53 days). The gravitational pull of the moon and the sun causes the tides. The moon's phases affect the amount of light available at night from full moon to new moon. Many organisms have rhythms that correspond to the lunar cycles.

From menstrual cycles to ocean tides, life on Earth resonates to a lunar rhythm. We live in lunar cycles of about twenty-eight days. These phases express lunar rhythms that we usually describe as months, although there is not a one-to-one correspondence with our current calendar.

Everywhere we find relics of mythic, mystic, romantic meanings—in the words *moonstruck* and *moonshine* and *lunatic* (in Latin, *luna* means "moon") and in the moonlight setting of lovers' meetings. The word *moon* in English (and its cognates in other languages) is rooted in the base meaning "measure" (as in Greek *metron* and English *meter* and *measure*).[10] It is worth figuring out how to flow our lives in these often overlooked lunar rhythms, because they are fundamental to our natural environment.

## WEEKLY (SABBATH) RHYTHMS

Though the week is the only chronos cycle without a basis in astronomical phenomena, in today's global culture we are keenly aware of the weekly rhythm with its "workdays" and "weekend." No one would name a restaurant TGIM ("Thank God It's Monday").

Our lives are structured largely around a weekly pattern. Indeed, as Pitirim Sorokin observed, the week is "one of the most important points in our 'orientation' in time and social reality."[11] As children, we learn the meaning of a weekend before we learn the meaning of a month.

Most cultures use the concept of a week, sometimes of varying lengths.[12] But where did the week come from? In *The Seven Day Circle: The History and the Meaning of the Week,* Eviatar Zerubavel explains how the concept of the week evolved from religion, holy numbers, planets, and astrology—hence our shortened labels for Saturn Day, Sun Day, and Moon Day.[13] Some numbers are considered desirable, lucky, or holy in many cultures; the number seven is one of these. This is one reason why there are seven days in the week (in fact, in many languages the word for "week" is synonymous with the word for "seven").

Our lives are structured largely around a weekly pattern. . . . We learn the meaning of a weekend before we learn the meaning of a month.

Weekly rhythms are one of the more puzzling and fascinating scientific findings in chronobiology because there is no direct astronomical correlation with the seven-day period as there is with the day, the month, the year, and the seasons. However, some scientists have discovered surprising biological bases for a seven-day cycle.

According to Susan Perry and Jim Dawson in *The Secrets Our Body Clocks Reveal,* "At first glance, it might seem that weekly rhythms developed in response to the seven-day week imposed by human culture thousands of years ago. However, this theory doesn't hold once you realize that plants, insects, and animals other than humans also have weekly cycles. . . . Biology, therefore, not culture, is probably at the source of our seven-day week."[14]

Jeremy Campbell, in his fascinating book *Winston Churchill's*

*Afternoon Nap*, summarizes the findings of the world's foremost authority on rhythms and the pioneer of the science of chronobiology: "Franz Halberg proposes that body rhythms of about seven days, far from being passively driven by the social cycle of the calendar week, are innate, autonomous, and perhaps the reason why the calendar week arose in the first place."[15]

The rhythm of a Sabbath is ancient. It was Hebrew culture that gave us the concept. God created the world in six days and rested on the seventh. Jews, Christians, and Muslims, with their three different holy days—Saturday, Sunday, and Friday, respectively—have each helped spread the seven-day week to the world. Few people practice a traditional Sabbath rest, but perhaps we need to bring that back into our lives as a healthy weekly rhythm.

### DAILY (CIRCADIAN) RHYTHMS

During the 1980s, huge advances were made in understanding daily, or circadian (*circ*, "about"; *diem*, "a day"), rhythms, which are based on the cycle of light and dark. As a result of the Earth's spin on its axis, we have the solar day (approximately twenty-four hours), which is responsible for the generation of other twenty-four-hour rhythms, one of the most significant of these being the light/dark cycle. Circadian rhythms have received notice in the popular press because the rhythm of light and dark has such an effect on us. From sleep to personal hygiene, the flow of a day governs regular life rituals.

Few people practice a traditional Sabbath rest, but perhaps we need to bring that back into our lives as a healthy weekly rhythm.

Studies on circadian rhythms are commonly applied to sleep disorders, jet lag, and shift workers (e.g., nurses, police officers, computer programmers, stockers, bakers, musicians). Commonly, organisms are asleep and awake for a certain time each day, and the sleep/wake pattern is repeated day after day, forming a rhythm. Many organisms also show a body temperature rhythm, where their core temperature fluctuates over a twenty-four-hour period, and this fluctuation is repeated day after day. When we violate natural daily rhythms in our 24/7, always-lit-up world, we suffer consequences. For instance, if we do not get enough sleep, we will be exhausted and find it hard to concentrate or to control our temper. We get grumpy! Others also suffer the consequences of our violation of the daily cycle.

When we violate natural daily rhythms in our 24/7, always-lit-up world, we suffer consequences.

The phases of the day are well-known: sunrise, morning, midmorning, midday (usually lunchtime), midafternoon (for some, a siesta time or tea time), evening (usually including dinner), sunset, and night. Without the other rhythms as context, we misuse most of our days. In the context of the longer rhythms, we can relax about what we are *not* doing in a given day. If we try to be totally balanced in any particular day, we really get in a mess, piling on unnecessary stress. To live rhythmically, we must consider all five created rhythms—annual, seasonal, monthly, weekly, daily—in harmony with one another.

Each society, subculture, family, and person builds unique daily rituals, but we all have them, and many are common to all. Few people go a day without brushing their teeth. Some would not think of missing a cup of coffee, watching CNN or ESPN, interacting on Facebook, or reading their Bible.

Part of the reason for our high stress levels is that we ignore the basic cycles of our planet. Fighting those rhythms creates frustration because the rhythms don't change; instead, we begin to burn out. In a crazy, senseless syndrome, we feel guilty because we cannot overcome natural cycles by sleeping less or maintaining a consistent lifestyle. But natural rhythms were never meant to be overcome; instead, we are meant to harmonize our life with them. You can find freedom from much of your guilt, stress, burnout, and excessive busyness by learning how to follow the sky, the natural cycles generated by the sun, moon, and Earth.

In the next three chapters, we will consider three chronos rhythm strategies that will enable you to make your life flow in sync with the five chronos cycles and thus live a better life!

# 10 Chronos Strategy #1: Pace Yourself

*I can't think about that right now. If I do, I'll go crazy. I'll think about that tomorrow. . . . Tara! Home. I'll go home. And I'll think of some way to get him back. After all . . . tomorrow is another day.*

SCARLETT O'HARA, *GONE WITH THE WIND*

I may not be a runner, but I know that you don't run a marathon at the same speed you run the 100-meter dash. Your pace varies significantly from an 800-meter race to a mile run to a 10K. Each race requires its own distinct pace. If you try to sprint a mile, you will quickly exhaust yourself and collapse. I'd fall on my face after the first two hundred yards.

## Set an Appropriate Frequency

In our day-to-day lives, however, most of us are trying to run every race at the same pace. Then we feel guilty and stressed when we can't do it. Each of the five chronos cycles has an inherent pace. Matching that pace—or setting the appropriate frequency—is the key to learning how to flow with it well. If that sounds difficult to imagine, let me remind you that we live in these cycles already. The question is, how well do we understand them and flow with them? Learning to flow with chronos cycles will bring more peace into your life.

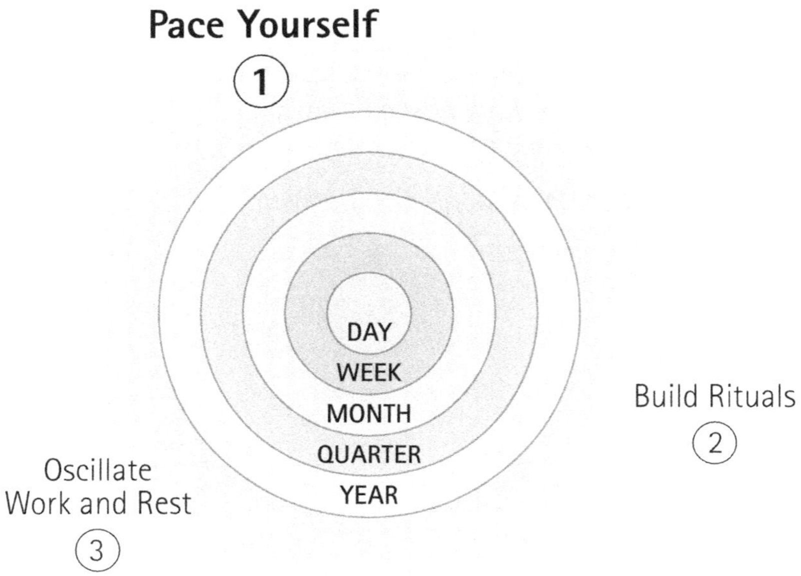


## SYLLABUS SHOCK

I remember being a freshman at the University of Texas in Austin and how it felt the first week of school when I encountered syllabus shock. Syllabus shock comes from laying out all the work for an entire semester based on the syllabus for each class. Although I knew better rationally, I felt as if I had twenty books to read, fifteen tests to take, seven papers to write, and three labs to do—*right then!* I had to force myself to imagine spreading all this work over the next fifteen weeks.

Most of us live our lives in syllabus shock—constantly putting before us every assignment from every course in life. That pressure induces guilt, stress, and condemnation. We need to learn how to envision longer rhythms of time, such as a semester.

We will find more peaceful, enjoyable, and fulfilled lives if we can identify appropriate frequencies for our regular activities. "Today" may not be the day for Scarlett to think of a way to get Rhett Butler back. When we try to balance all our obligations every week, we ignore the benefits of longer rhythms. When our lives are in a good rhythm, we can relax about the pressure of "imbalance" in a given week because we know we are achieving a healthy pace over the course of a year, though it may not be evident in one particular week.

We will find more peaceful, enjoyable, and fulfilled lives if we can identify appropriate frequencies for our regular activities.

We need to find the best frequency, the best pace, for each activity and appreciate the flow of our cycles. Last week, my daughter called from Baylor University. She said she was disappointed in herself because she was not getting any studying done on Tuesdays. She was expecting that she should study the same amount every day (a balance mentality), but Tuesdays were throwing her off because she had classes all day and into the evening. When we discussed various rhythm strategies (to free her from the burden of balance), she realized that Tuesdays should not be a study day; Wednesdays, when she is done with her classes before noon, could be a major study day. By releasing expectations and bringing her study schedule into harmony with the rhythm of her class schedule, Melanie was able to relieve stress and frustration and get all her work done in a timely manner.

## PAYING BILLS

Establishing good intervals can release stress. For instance, you may be able to pay your bills in a single evening once a month, and yet because you haven't established this monthly rhythm, you live with the daily pressure that you should be taking care of the bills. If you put "pay bills" on your daily to-do list and feel undue condemnation every day that you do not cross it off your list, you only add to your stress and frustration. Why not pick one day a month that you will pay the bills? Then live all the other days of the month in freedom, knowing that bill-paying day will come and that it is the only day you need to bear the responsibility of paying the bills.

A woman named Jane heard me teach this truth a few years ago. Later, she came back and told me that she now pays her bills online. She spent a few hours one day setting up the online bill-paying feature on her bank's Web site, and now she's able to easily pay her bills one day a month. She said it has made her life so much easier.

A few months later, I received the following e-mail from Jane: "A funny thing happened today. I started to panic, thinking I had not paid my bills on time. So I went to my online banking site, and then I realized I had already entered the automatic bill pay, so I don't have to worry about them for the rest of the year. Thanks! That was a great (simple) stress- and time-relieving suggestion."

> We experience too much confusion and stress when we try to force longer rhythms into shorter cycles.

We experience too much confusion and stress when we try to force longer rhythms into shorter cycles—living daily with feelings of guilt because we have not called Mom, when that is a weekly task we could do on Sundays, or feeling guilty because we haven't cleaned the garage, when that is a seasonal task that we can plan to do two months from now (and not worry about it until then).

It's like doing our taxes. Most of us don't worry on a daily basis about filing our income taxes—we know that's an annual task we'll accomplish in an evening or two of intense work sometime between the end of January (when the W-2s arrive in the mail) and April 15 (when we have until midnight to postmark our returns).

To live in harmony with each rhythm—annual, seasonal, monthly, weekly, daily—we should ask, What's the best frequency for each activity, task, and responsibility in my life? Is this something to do daily, weekly, monthly, seasonally, or annually? How often will we strip the wood floors, dust the shelves, do laundry, clean the gutters, go on a date with our spouses, spend time with God, read a book, spend a few hours with the kids, go to church services, attend a spiritual conference, take a vacation, eat dessert, or go out for dinner?

Few people I've spoken to have considered an appropriate pace for each of the varied activities and responsibilities they bear. Instead, by trying to keep all their obligations in constant balance, they're wearing themselves out. Most people overfocus on the day and the week to the neglect of the longer rhythms.

If we can learn to follow the simple rhythm strategy of pacing ourselves, we will find more peace in our lives. We will be able to release ourselves from the unconscious pressure of all our responsibilities coming to bear at one time.

## Follow the Flow of Each Chronos Cycle

Each cycle carries an inherent flow. Though the cycle itself is universal, the flow of life generated by the cycle varies by such factors as culture, geography, personal seasons, and stage of life. It is valuable to consider the flow of your life in these cycles. (See appendix A for an exercise that will help you identify the flow of your chronos cycles.)

### ANNUAL CYCLES

We live in orbital cycles, but we have paid little attention to this rhythm because most time-management systems focus primarily on the day and the week. What events, activities, and celebrations recur annually, but not daily, weekly, monthly, or quarterly? Think through different categories. Look through the lens of each of your stewardships.

We live in orbital cycles, but most time-management systems focus primarily on the day and the week.

Holidays recur annually, as do taxes and anniversaries. Anniversaries may mark the dates not only of weddings but of major events such as the death of a family member, the start of an organization, or historic world events like D-day or 9/11. It sounds crazy, but every year many people are surprised by the advent of an annual event. "Oh my goodness, it's Christmas already. I haven't bought any gifts!" "Is your birthday *next* week?!" But by anticipating the annual recurrence of certain cycles, we gain the opportunity to reframe our experience.

### QUARTERLY CYCLES

Unlike the other chronos cycles, a quarterly cycle carries less recurrence and more uniqueness. Each season brings a unique flavor to life. Winter, spring, summer, and fall give us their own special weather and colors. Because seasons do not recur quarterly, annual and seasonal cycles are best considered together.

What takes place on a seasonal or quarterly basis? Financial reports from companies, economic data, and taxes, to name just a few. We open investment reports each quarter to smile in satisfaction or hit the table in frustration. School grading periods roughly conform to quarters. In business, people commonly plan in quarters: bonuses, goals, and stock reports come quarterly. In our personal lives, few of us think in quarters; yet it is useful to do so. It works well to plan your life on a quarterly basis.

### MONTHLY CYCLES

In thinking of an entire month at a time, it is helpful to focus on the weekends. How will you invest the four or five Saturdays and Sundays of the month? What activities recur monthly, but not annually, quarterly, weekly, or daily? Think about balancing bank accounts, appointments for health and hygiene, and entertainment.

### WEEKLY AND DAILY CYCLES

Most management systems focus on daily and weekly rhythms, so they are better understood than other cycles. It is helpful to think of a week in twenty-one time segments: the morning, afternoon, and evening of seven days. How have you apportioned those times based on your values and responsibilities? (For a chart of various activities arranged according to each of the five cycles, see appendix A on chronos cycles and life scheduling. This appendix explains the twenty-one-segment approach, along with other scheduling ideas.)

## WHEN CYCLES DON'T MESH

One major source of conflict in relationships comes from differing expectations about the frequency of important activities. If you run with a partner, for instance, you need to talk about your pace. If you are married, how often will you have a date night or get away, just the two of you? Weekly, monthly, annually? How often will you give each other a small gift? How often will each of you spend time with your own friends, apart from your spouse? I often talk with couples who have not taken a vacation with just the two of them in years. They have not had one evening alone together in months. Early in our marriage, vacations were a major issue between Tamara and me. We simply had different values and different expectations based on our experiences growing up. In my family, when we took a vacation, it meant we went on a trip. In Tamara's family, vacations were times for getting projects done around the house, such as stripping and waxing the floors each spring.

One major source of conflict in relationships comes from differing expectations about the frequency of important activities.

For me, travel vacations are a necessity; for Tamara, they are a luxury. Practically, that means we anticipate vacations on different cycles. I anticipate a few vacations each year, including weekend getaways. Tamara anticipates a travel vacation every few years, sprinkled between major "honey do" projects around the house. For years, we were running at different paces. Finally, we sat down and talked through our differences. We found it helped to understand the other person's perspective and to acknowledge that we were different. Then we worked together to arrive at a compromise pace we could both accept.

Ideally, couples will create marital rhythms in each of the

five chronos cycles. You may eat a meal together weekly, have a date together monthly, and take a vacation without the kids annually. Share your expectations with each other. Too often, we live with unnecessary guilt, with a vague feeling that we are not giving enough time to our relationships. Why? Because we have not talked through our expectations and learned to pace ourselves together.

## Case Study: Jaime and Yesinia Gonzalez

Over lunch at a local café, Jaime Gonzalez shared his heart with me. Along with his wife, Yesinia, and their two small children, Jaime recently moved from the San Francisco Bay area to Dallas. Their life mission is to serve God in full-time ministry. They are committed to making the necessary sacrifices for Jaime to get the education he needs to serve as a pastor.

Jaime was greatly concerned. He told me that Yesinia was now waving the red flag. With Yesinia working full-time in medical records, and Jaime working part-time to start a Spanish-speaking service at a church as well as going to school full-time, they rarely see each other, much less have any quality time together. Yesinia leaves for work before Jaime gets up. He gets home from school after she is asleep. During the week, they either have obligations or Jaime must study. What can they do?

Rather than diagnosing their problem as being "out of balance," I see the issue as not living in a good rhythm. Could they develop marriage-strengthening habits in each of the five cycles by considering their frequency and flow?

Starting with the daily pace, I asked Jaime if he and Yesinia could adjust their morning routines so that they see each other for at least fifteen minutes each day to touch base.

They could share coffee together or dress together or pray together to connect.

We also looked for a period of time they could reserve for each other on a weekly cycle. Jaime was studying on Sunday nights to be ready for assignments due Monday, but he realized he could wait to study until after Yesinia was asleep. They reserved two hours on Sunday nights to spend together as a couple. They arranged for Jaime's parents to watch the kids during that time each week. Even when the rest of the week was busy, Jaime and Yesinia knew they could count on this time together on Sundays.

Addressing the monthly chronos cycle, I encouraged Jaime to set aside a day to spend with his family, even if he had to miss a class at school or he and Yesinia had to take one day a month off from work. Many months already have days off built in—such as Presidents' Day, Memorial Day, Independence Day, and Labor Day. Jaime and Yesinia picked these monthly days in advance and blocked them out on the calendar for each other and their family. Again, even if the rest of their schedule was filled with other obligations, they both knew they could count on one day a month to be together as a family with no other distractions or obligations.

I asked Jaime if seasonally (once every three months) he could give a weekend (two or three days) to Yesinia and the children. When he and I looked at the calendar, we realized that such times already existed with Thanksgiving break, Christmas break, and spring break. In some seasons, he might have to be more intentional about finding a full weekend, but he saw that it was possible. He also realized that he and Yesinia could probably reserve one long weekend a quarter for just themselves as well.

Finally, we looked at the entire year. Once a year, could

they take a weeklong vacation as a family? Jaime was sure that was possible. The budget would dictate the nature of the vacation, but they could take the time. By putting the vacation on the calendar, Jaime knew that Yesinia and the children would have that week to look forward to far in advance.

When Jaime went home and shared this rhythmic plan with Yesinia, she lowered the red flag. Though nothing had changed in their work and school responsibilities, they could envision a livable pace in their relationship. The secret was not trying to achieve an artificial ideal of balance, but to seek to live in rhythm with their natural chronos cycles. Instead of trying to manage their time, Jaime and Yesinia learned to flow in harmony with the cycles already built into the world.

**Jaime and Yesinia Gonzalez' Rhythmic Plan for a Healthy Marriage**

*Frequency or Pace*

**Daily:** Fifteen minutes of morning connection time

**Weekly:** Two hours of Sunday evening couple time, with no kids

**Monthly:** One full day together as a family

**Quarterly:** One long weekend as a family

**Annually:** One weeklong vacation as a family

Yesinia and Jaime discovered a life rhythm that promised less guilt, less stress, and no burnout. On the flip side, they gained more hope, harmony, and happiness. Now they are living in tune with the natural cycles that create the rhythm of their lives. You can experience the same kind of breakthrough in your own life.

## Applying the Strategy to Your Relationship with God: Devotional Paces

As I was growing up, my parents took my siblings and me to church on Sundays. There we learned that we should have a daily "quiet time" with God. How do you do that? I was told to read my Bible and pray. Later, people gave all kinds of suggestions about how to keep the time fresh, including listening to worship music, reading a devotional book, meditating, memorizing Scripture, taking a walk, reading different sections of the Bible, and journaling.

I was never sure how long my quiet time was supposed to last. One booklet talked about seven minutes with God; another one described an hour of prayer. A biography of Martin Luther said that the busier he was, the longer he spent alone with God. It seemed that the more spiritual I wanted to be, the more time I would spend in "quiet time." I almost felt like it was a competition. Maybe that's not what's intended, but in some circles it happens. "How much time did *you* spend with God today?"

If God has placed us in a world that is governed by certain rhythms, it seems natural to relate to him in a rhythmic way.

After my trip to New Zealand, as I began to develop the concept of rhythm, I asked myself, *Why not think rhythmically about the time I spend with God?* If God has placed us in a world that is governed by certain rhythms, it seems natural to relate to him in a rhythmic way.

As I continued to spend time with God in his Word, I began to prayerfully consider how to live well in each changing season, and I began to develop five devotional paces to match the five natural chronos rhythms of life. Apart from the times I would normally spend in sermon preparation, study, and prayer opportunities at McKinney Fellowship, I decided to implement the following rhythms for my personal quiet time with God:

**Daily:** Fifteen minutes of prayer and Bible reading
**Weekly:** Half hour of prayer and meditation on Scripture
**Monthly:** One hour of prayer and meditation on Scripture
**Quarterly:** Three hours of spiritual reflection and planning
**Annually:** One full day of spiritual retreat, including reflection on the previous year and setting plans for the coming year

As you seek to harmonize your life in the five chronos cycles, you will see a difference, even by making just a small start. It is easy to get overwhelmed because this is new and you haven't done it before. But it really isn't new. It's the way people have lived since the dawn of time. It is only within the past hundred years or so that our artificial, modern, technological, 24/7 world has distanced us from a more simple, enjoyable, and sustainable way of life, one in harmony with chronos cycles.

This is the way life works best. When our lives don't flow with the created chronos cycles, we encounter stress because we are violating the basic structure of our world. A much better way to live is to move toward understanding and living in harmony with the cycles.

Take at least one simple step. Realize that you cannot do everything at once, or all at one pace. Different activities have their appropriate frequencies. Resolve to reduce your stress in accordance with the five chronos cycles. By adopting a rhythm strategy, you will reconnect to the natural cycles of our world.

By pacing yourself with the way life works, you can reduce burnout and busyness. Guilt can be released by freeing yourself from the false expectation that you must carry all of life's responsibilities every day. That is a heavy burden we were never intended to carry. Find the best frequency for the activities in your life. Relax. Let each cycle have its natural flow in your life. In the next two chapters, we will look more specifically at how you can build life-enhancing rituals into each cycle (which will increase your fulfillment), and how to oscillate between work and rest (which is the secret to sustaining a rhythmic pattern throughout your life).

By pacing yourself with the way life works, you can reduce burnout and busyness.

---

LIFE EXERCISE: *Try the following steps to help you get started with pacing yourself:*

1. *Change the frequency of one activity in your life to a more appropriate pace.*
2. *Take one aspect of your life and consider paces that follow the flow of the natural chronos cycles. (See Jaime and Yesinia's story for ideas.)*
3. *Talk about your pace with those you live with.*

# Life Exercise:

*Identify the frequency of the activities in your life*

| Activities | Frequency | | | | |
|---|---|---|---|---|---|
| | YEARLY | QUARTERLY | MONTHLY | WEEKLY | DAILY |
| *Wash the dog* | | | × | | |
| *Vacuum* | | | | × | |
| *Christmas shop* | × | | | | |
| *Call Mom* | | | | | × |
| *Call brother* | | | | × | |
| | | | | | |
| | | | | | |
| | | | | | |
| | | | | | |
| | | | | | |
| | | | | | |
| | | | | | |
| | | | | | |
| | | | | | |
| | | | | | |
| | | | | | |
| | | | | | |
| | | | | | |

# 11

# Chronos Strategy #2: Build Rituals

*Coordinated repetition creates cohesion.*

Burnout does not result from hard work. When we are achieving what is important to us, we are fulfilled. Merely slowing down and taking more downtime will not grant you a better life. It might actually give you a boring life or an insignificant one. If you are feeling burned out or unfulfilled, there are other factors at work.

When you shift foundations to a rhythmic paradigm for living, you can implement powerful strategies for a better life. In addition to pacing yourself for greater peace, you can build life-enhancing rituals for more fulfillment.

Building life-enhancing rituals is a powerful strategy

that works in the flow of life's natural cycles. When Jaime and Yesinia Gonzalez began to set aside time for each other and their family, they were beginning to establish marital and family rituals that would enable them to experience less stress and more peace, less frustration and more joy, less ineffectiveness and more fruitfulness.

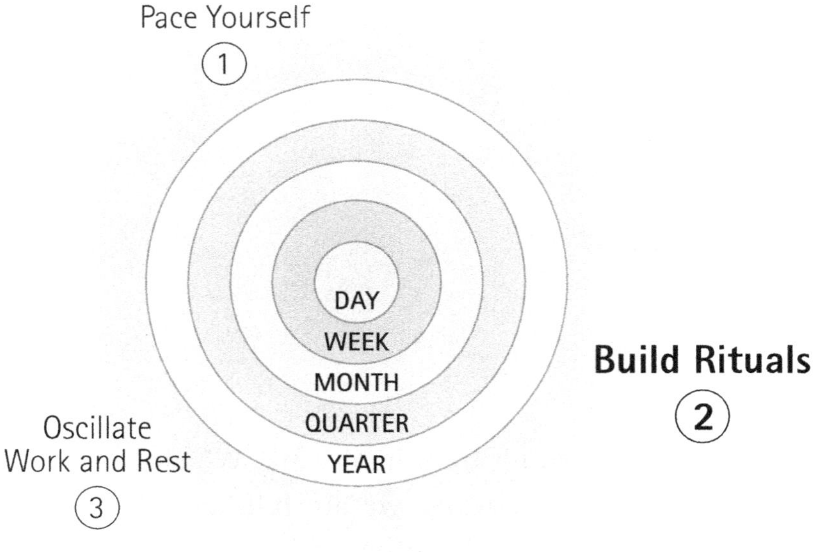


What is a ritual? Depending on your life experience, the term *ritual* will conjure up a wide variety of connotations. My son David and his girlfriend immediately think about their fraternity and sorority handshakes and songs. In contrast, my son Jimmy, who works for a sports radio station, starts telling stories about bizarre pregame warm-up activities. As a pastor, I think about baptism and Communion. Sociologists define *rituals* as repeated activities that create meaning in a culture. Marriage and family Web sites list dozens of family rituals to enhance relationships.

In *The Power of Full Engagement*, Jim Loehr and Tony Schwartz include a chapter titled "Taking Action: The Power of Positive Rituals." Their research reveals how rituals have enabled top athletes to perform at consistently high levels. For Loehr and Schwartz, a ritual can be any healthy routine, though sociologists tend to distinguish routines from rituals based on the assumption that rituals are connected to some deeper meaning or significance.

Rituals have the power to help us achieve our mission in every area of our lives.

Rituals have the power to help us achieve our mission in every area of our lives. They can be communal, involving a team, community, or family, and they can also be personal. For a richer understanding of ritual, consider its use in multiple human arenas.

In certain contexts, *ritual* refers to a prescribed order in a religious ceremony. But *ritual* also means "a detailed method or procedure faithfully or regularly followed; or a state or condition characterized by the presence of established procedure or routine."[1]

For some people, *ritual* and *tradition* are synonymous. Traditions are characteristic patterns, methods, or beliefs often passed down over a long period of time. Though distinctions between traditions and rituals can be made, their meanings often overlap. Rituals can have little sense of "belief," but the action may signify a belief.

Sociologist William Doherty defines three characteristics of ritual:

> Rituals are social interactions that are repeated, coordinated, and significant. This is the classical, anthropological definition going back to [Arnold] van Gennep's work in 1908. Rituals can be everyday interactions, or they could be once a year, but they're repeated. They're also coordinated. You have to know what is expected of you in a ritual; you can't have a meal ritual together if you don't know when to show up for it, and you can't dance together if you don't know what kind of dance you are going to do. You're not going to have much of a sexual life if you don't end up in the same space at the same time. Rituals are not only repeated and coordinated, they are significant. A ritual is something that has positive emotional meaning to both parties.[2]

The period of time is not a crucial element, but a ritual is repeated, coordinated, and significant. In this case, Doherty is thinking of ritual in ways that involve only more than one person. Personal rituals need not be coordinated.

## The Personal Power of Ritual

In contrast, Loehr and Schwartz define a ritual as simply a routine, repeated action. For them, positive rituals are "precise, consciously acquired behaviors that become *automatic* in our lives, fueled by deep purpose."[3] Routines can translate our values into action and embody them. For an athlete, practice makes perfect.

Loehr and Schwartz correctly point out that rituals must be most rigorous when the challenge is most exacting, such as when soldiers are preparing for war. The United States Marine Corps builds rituals into teenagers to turn them into Marines ready to perform under the most extreme conditions. In this sense, rituals are similar to what Stephen Covey calls *habits.* In a spiritual or business context, we might use the word *disciplines* to describe personal rituals.

## The Social Power of Rituals

As social beings, we like to do things together, whether it is celebrating, grieving, or remembering. Collective activity reinforces group solidarity. Whether we are talking about a Memorial Day parade, a Roman Catholic mass, or an annual quilting bee, rituals have the power to build communal identity and reinforce values.

Because rituals are so ancient and universal, some people believe they are a way of making contact with our subconscious in powerful ways. Perhaps they touch a fundamental need in human nature. According to Dr. John D. Friesen, professor of family studies in the Department of Counseling Psychology at the University of British Columbia, studies have suggested a neurological connection with rituals.[4]

Rituals and traditions enable families to build memories and pass on cultural identity and value to succeeding generations.

Rituals and traditions enable families to build memories and pass on cultural identity and value to succeeding generations. This happens with patriotism as well, such as when we salute the flag, say the Pledge of Allegiance, and stand for the national anthem. Rituals strengthen human communities.

## The Power of Ritual for Families

In addition to his role as a professor, William Doherty has written extensively on the value of ritual for families and marriages. As author of *The Intentional Family*, he helped found Family Life First, "a grassroots community organization dedicated to restoring the primacy of family time." *Parent News* interviewed him about his work on the role of family rituals in strengthening family ties.

> **Parent News:** In your writings about the American family in modern society, you contrast the intentional family—one that creates and maintains a sense of connection, meaning, and community—with the entropic family—one that loses a sense of cohesion over the years through lack of conscious attention to its inner life and community ties. What role do rituals play in the intentional family?
>
> **William Doherty:** Rituals are crucial for busy modern family members to connect with one another. Without regular times to be together as a family, interacting with conversation, play, or other activities, families drift apart. Families float south on the river unless they paddle.[5]

Doherty emphasized that such rituals are especially crucial for adolescents, who polls show are heavily concerned about family time. Without it, teenagers run the risk of living lives parallel to the rest of the family.

Rituals may also play a protective role in families facing other disruptive issues. For instance, in families with an alcoholic member, the deliberate planning and preservation of family rituals, specifically dinnertime, protected the children from developing problematic drinking patterns. Patients with chronic pain reported more satisfaction with family life when predictable and organized routines were part of their daily activities. Children with asthma were less likely to experience anxiety symptoms when their families engaged in meaningful rituals.[6]

A compelling article in the American Psychological Association's *Journal of Family Psychology* demonstrates the crucial importance of rituals to the health and well-being of families trying to balance work and home in today's busy, stress-filled world. Rituals provide stability in times of stress and transition. They are associated with marital satisfaction, adolescents' sense of personal identity, children's health, academic achievement, and stronger family relationships. In their early years, children are healthier and their behavior is better regulated when there are predictable routines in the family. For instance, children with regular bedtime routines go to sleep sooner and wake up less frequently during the night than those with less regular routines.[7]

Despite all the obstacles to sitting down for a family meal, the repetitive nature of regular, shared mealtimes allows families to get to know each other better, which can lead to better parenting, healthier children, and improved academic performance. These kinds of simple rituals are disappearing in a nonrhythmic world.

Rituals provide stability in times of stress and transition.

What makes up a family ritual? Despite differences in socioeconomic status, ethnicity, and religion, rituals are found in all families. William Doherty emphasizes three ingredients that make up family rituals:

1. *Special meaning or significance.* Small things can meet this requirement: celebrating the first snow by building a snowman together, lying on the floor and

reading the Sunday funnies, Dad and the kids going for doughnuts on Saturday morning so Mom can sleep in. The cost or the amount of time spent is less important than the feeling that "this is special" or "this is something we like doing together."

2. *Repetition*. Doing something together once is wonderful, but it doesn't qualify as a ritual unless it's done again and again so that family members have a chance to look forward to the event. Both anticipation beforehand and pleasant memories afterward contribute to the value of family traditions.
3. *Coordination*. In order for an activity to be a genuine ritual, people must participate in it deliberately. Someone has to be sure it happens. The ideal, of course, is if different family members take the lead for different rituals. But someone needs to take charge and coordinate the event.[8]

We can build three general types of family rituals: holidays and rites of passage (arising from religious, cultural, or ethnic origins); traditions that symbolize a family value (possibly rooted in previous generations); and family routines that reflect unique interactions, often in shorter time spans. By using our understanding of the chronos cycles, we can apply the strategy of rituals in a more concrete and practical way. Use your grasp of each cycle's flow to build rituals personally, with your family, or in your workplace.

### MARRIAGE RITUALS

In his keynote address to the 2007 Smart Marriages Conference in Denver, Colorado, William Doherty gave a clear explanation of marriage rituals:

> I divide marriage rituals into rituals of connection, rituals of intimacy, and rituals of community. Examples of connection rituals include good-byes in the morning, greetings in the evening, and going out for coffee and conversation. I talked to a woman who said she and her husband always say "I love you" when they part in the morning, because they never know that they will see each other again. Working in the garden together can be a connection ritual. . . .
>
> Intimacy rituals include dates where you're going out to have some special time together, patterns of sexual intimacy, and special occasions such as anniversaries or Valentine's Day. By the way, I think anniversaries are the least intentionally celebrated ritual in the American family. You ask most people about their anniversaries, and they respond sheepishly that they don't do much for it. Anniversaries tend to occur on days like Tuesday, most of the rest of the world doesn't know about it, and there are kid events to go to. But anniversaries are really the birthday of our marriage, and we tend to let them go without much ritual. . . .
>
> Commitment to our rituals can provide the glue we need to stick together during the times of stress and the seasons of despair.[9]

As with personal, social, and family rituals, marriage rituals are repetitive and carry meaning or value. Because they are repetitive, it is easy to build rituals into the chronos cycles.

### WORSHIP RITUALS

Liturgical Christians have long benefited from an annual rhythm built into the church year. Lectionaries (liturgical readings) developed over centuries provide songs, readings, and prayers in a predictable cycle of spiritual renewal. More recently, younger Christians outside denominational structures are returning to ancient church practices, including liturgies and lectionaries.

Beginning in the centuries just after Christ, but more fully evolving in the Middle Ages, monastic communities developed daily and weekly rituals of spiritual health. Prayers according to the hours of the day, rhythms of worship and work, private and communal prayer, and times of meditation structured the lives of those in the monasteries. Today, a "New Monasticism" is rising up to promote the benefit of monastic rituals without having to actually live in a monastery.[10] You can focus your consideration of rituals by looking at them in longer and shorter cycles.

## Life-Enhancing Rituals in Longer Chronos Cycles

### BIRTHDAYS AND ANNIVERSARIES

The cycle of a year provides obvious opportunities for building value-creating rituals on holidays and birthdays. Even though we know they are coming, many of us find that birthdays and holidays sneak up on us.

Men are notorious for this. Many of us give little thought to birthdays and anniversaries until right before the date—if we even remember at all. My worst mistake was a few years ago now, but my stomach still knots up when I remember it. My anniversary is July 2, and Tamara's birthday is July 6. That year I forgot *both* of them! It was bad—I'm still paying for it. I'm hoping a rhythm approach to life will keep me from ever making that mistake again!

Tamara and I have five children. All day on their birthday, they get to eat from the "You're the Best" plate. We take it down from its place on the kitchen wall to celebrate them on their birthday. In your family, no matter what kind of family you have, you, too, can creatively develop traditions. It is never too late to start.

Seriously, we need to give much more thought to celebrating and commemorating special occasions. It's the thought that expresses the love, and it's rituals that ingrain values while building relationships.

> We need to give much more thought to celebrating and commemorating special occasions. Rituals ingrain values while building relationships.

### HOLIDAYS

"Whose family are we going to be with?" If you like conflict, it's a fun question to ask around the holidays. Couples argue every year over whom they will be spending time with for Thanksgiving and Christmas. But it doesn't have to be that way.

Holidays can be much less stressful when an annual cycle is considered far in advance. In premarital counseling, I help engaged couples think through how they are going to celebrate the holidays with their new in-laws. If you wait until the holidays are upon you, stress and tension can overwhelm you. Emotions can get the best of you. Make a plan in advance whom you will see on which holidays throughout the year. Build your rituals and communicate your plans far in advance.

Stage of life matters. Rituals don't last forever. For years when the children were young, we drove to a local fireworks display on Independence Day. When they became teenagers, we changed the tradition to buying our own fireworks. We drove out to a safe place to set them off. (Of course, you can't do this if fireworks are illegal in your state.) Now, with grown children, we don't usually do fireworks at all—we watch them on television.

Each year on Labor Day, before our kids were old enough to drive, we took the whole family to Sandy Lake Park, a low-budget amusement park with a huge swimming pool. We made a day of it, picnic lunch and all. It became a family ritual for at least a decade. Then its time was done.

In our family, during the weeks leading up to Christmas, we lit the candles on an Advent wreath. Each candle had a Bible story connected with it, as well as a Christmas carol. A different child would light the new candle each week. It was a big deal. We're thinking of restarting the ritual with our grandchildren someday. Some families drive around looking at Christmas lights and drinking eggnog. With rituals, it's the repetition that develops the memory and seals the value.

With rituals, it's the repetition that develops the memory and seals the value.

We have always opened presents on Christmas morning. In an attempt to break from materialism, last Christmas morning we started a new ritual of gathering around the tree for a special time of prayer, of remembering whom we are celebrating and why. The presents are a way of celebrating the Incarnation.

On Memorial Day, we've started a new ritual of going to a ceremony at a historic local cemetery where veterans from several wars are buried. For my father, a Marine Corps veteran, Memorial Day is a significant day, and he has developed his own personal traditions. First, he has determined not to buy anything on Memorial Day because the day has not been set aside to shop. Instead, he displays the American and Marine Corps flags on his front porch, and he uses the day to sit on his back patio and call old Marine buddies. Later, he pays a visit to the local veterans cemetery and places single red roses tied with the Marine Corps ribbon on the graves of his fallen comrades, some he knew and others he didn't. He says, "These are the guys I couldn't call from my patio." He says a prayer over each grave, praying for strength for the surviving families, and then he thanks God for each of the brave men who gave their lives for our country.

### FOOD RITUALS

I love food. Food is always a big part of traditions. Of course, there is the Thanksgiving turkey, but there can be so much more. Tamara makes tortilla soup almost every Christmas Eve. On Christmas Day, we always eat nut bread from an old family recipe. Some friends of ours prefer to enjoy special occasions at a favorite restaurant.

The idea is to develop rituals that enable you to fulfill your mission.

Food can be part of traditions in the workplace, as well. In some companies, the annual picnic is a highlight. Cake and ice cream are almost always an appropriate way to celebrate birthdays at work. A department or team lunch can be a great way to celebrate meeting or exceeding goals. Get creative with food rituals.

### CAMPING

The idea is to develop rituals that enable you to fulfill your mission. Part of my mission involves parenting well. When my children were small, we bought camping gear. With only limited financial resources, most of our vacations involved camping in tents in various state parks. In retrospect, it was a huge blessing. With no distractions, we spent extended time enjoying each other. From all our camping adventures, we have great memories and lots of funny stories.

My kids tell the tale of the time I took the family up into

the mountains of New Mexico outside Red River. It got really cold. That night, the kids slept in the Suburban with our black Labrador retriever. By morning, the car doors were frozen shut. Though I wanted to stay, I got outvoted. The next night, we slept in a heated cabin in town.

As the children grew old enough to get summer jobs, planning a family vacation with everyone at the same time became more difficult. But that's part of the natural rhythm of life. Children grow up. During the years when your kids are under your roof, if at all possible take an annual family vacation.

### "THE PROGRAM"

My extended family has an amazing and unusual Thanksgiving tradition. Aunts, uncles, and cousins–including many in-laws–have gathered in Texas every year for about the last one hundred years. Often the group swells to fifty or seventy-five people. Nearly a century ago, one of the matriarchs started "The Program." This consists of every child, from very young ones to seniors in high school, sharing a talent, poem, or meaningful moment with the whole family. It works great for the little ones, but older kids hate it. Every year, the parents get all worked up over what their children are going to do for it. I was glad to graduate from high school just to get out of doing The Program on Thanksgiving. But of course I make my kids do it!

Between Christmas and New Year's, one family puts on a board game tournament, another family settles in for their annual movie-watching marathon, another works a giant jigsaw puzzle together, another plays a family flag football game. The sky's the limit. Come up with your own ideas and start creating some memorable traditions.

### PERSONAL RITUALS

To grow as a person, I take three days each year to be alone at a friend's lake house. It is a personal spiritual retreat, a time of prayer, fasting, reflection, and looking to what's ahead. Most years, I take advantage of some ongoing training to improve my skills and knowledge. On Labor Day weekend, I go on a Colorado Rocky Mountain adventure with two of my best friends, Mike and Bart.

Others I know take on a major project each year. Many people make a yearly pilgrimage to a sporting event: the Grand Prix, Super Bowl, World Series, Indy 500, or the Masters. For others, it is an entertainment ritual: a concert, festival, or show that happens each year. Seasonal changes bring other annual rituals, such as going to see the colorful autumn leaves in New England, or the wildflowers blooming in the spring, or whale watching off the Pacific coast. Others enter annual tournaments and competitions, which is not only a ritual in itself but also typically has many smaller rituals built into the experience.

> By building rituals in an annual cycle, you are achieving your mission in harmony with the way our world actually works.

By building rituals in an annual cycle, you will experience greater peace, joy, and fulfillment because you are achieving your mission in harmony with the way our world actually works. These cycles exist whether you pay attention to them or not. But when you live in harmony with them, you discover greater freedom from stress and burnout. You can relax and enjoy more of life.

## Life-Enhancing Rituals in Shorter Chronos Cycles

Months, weeks, and days offer shorter cycles in which to build life-enhancing rituals that enable you to accomplish more of what really matters. Rituals ensure that we use as little conscious energy as possible, leaving us free to strategically focus the energy available to us in creative, enriching ways.[11]

When we are young, we have to be taught to brush our teeth. Some of us fought that ritual and had to be reminded time after time. By now, as adults, brushing our teeth has become so ritualistic that we can do it half asleep, and we almost never forget to do it. Remembering to brush our teeth takes almost no mental energy because it is a ritual. Ritualizing behavior conserves mental energy and willpower for other tasks.

### MONTHLY RITUALS

As you think about the lunar cycle, imagine monthly rituals that could enhance your life. Could you establish a monthly visit with your grandparents that would help fulfill an aspect of your life's mission? Could you develop a physical or mental health ritual that would sustain, renew, and strengthen you? Perhaps a monthly drive to the lake or a walk in the park or the countryside?

One year, I developed the ritual of a monthly gift for Tamara. Each month, I picked out a different small gift: flowers, chocolate, bubble bath, and so forth. She appreciated it. Unfortunately, I have broken that habit and need to reestablish it.

If you have young children, you know they appreciate ritual. They love to anticipate events they can count on. If you don't already know that kids love repetition and recurrence, just watch *Blue's Clues* for a week. As a parent, you can develop monthly rituals that build life-giving joy into your children and your relationship with them. Some families enjoy a pancake breakfast once a month on a Saturday; others have a game night or movie night. Some go to the farmer's market or flea market once a month.

Imagine how a monthly ritual could strengthen your extended family. If they live nearby, perhaps you could develop a monthly family dinner together. If they live too far away, you could establish a monthly conference call instead.

In your personal and professional life, you can develop healthy rituals that will give you a better life. At work, every month you could meet personally with each person on your team. At home, discipline yourself to begin a financial ritual, such as balancing the bank account, or a cleaning ritual, such as dusting the house. Choose to do one home project monthly.

### WEEKLY RITUALS

Focus on discretionary time, such as evenings and weekends. Much of a weekly cycle is dictated by others. Your employer requires you to be on the job or working from home during certain hours. Your school expects you to be in class. As a mom, you have to be there for your children during certain hours. But what choices are you making with your discretionary time?

What creative weekly rituals could you build for effective, fruitful living? For instance, what could you do weekly to sustain your health as a family member? What could you do in your relationship with God? Weekly church attendance is slipping in America, but that's a ritual we don't want to lose. Some couples choose to enjoy a weekly date night, especially when the kids are school age.

What creative weekly rituals could you build for effective, fruitful living?

Many aspects of our lives are weekly. And yet there is a

big difference between passively stumbling through the weekly rhythm and intentionally setting up weekly rituals that will enhance your life.

## DAILY RITUALS

Rituals of greeting occur daily. As a young married couple, we bought a black Lab. When I came home from work, Glory bounded to the door, tail wagging, eyes looking up at me expectantly, so thankful to have me home. Tamara's greeting was not quite as enthusiastic, and one day I made a comment about it. The next day, Tamara determined to beat Glory to the door and top the dog's enthusiasm. We laugh about it now, but we still take time to say good-bye to each other when we part for a time and greet each other when we meet up again. A simple kiss and "I love you" can be a powerful ritual over thousands of days.

Rituals have great power on a daily cycle. For instance, if you want to keep abreast of current international events to be a good global citizen, develop the ritual of reading the daily international section on a news Web site. Schedule rituals into your daily pace. How will you connect with God, your spouse, children, or friends on a daily basis?

> Rituals have great power on a daily cycle. . . . Schedule rituals into your daily pace.

Because we eat every day, food and drink are helpful in building daily rituals. My wife and I share coffee together every morning. Most evenings we share dinner together as well.

Physical exercise rituals work well on a daily cycle, whether it's taking a walk, going to the gym, stretching, or calisthenics. Prayer, meditation, and reading Scripture are good daily rituals.

It is important to plan rituals for the daily cycle, but we must be careful that we put them in the context of the longer cycles. It is easy to overpack days when the old "balance monster" tells us we must give attention to every dimension of our lives right now. If you try to live "balanced" every day, you will go crazy. Though daily rituals are valuable, your days can and should be very different. One day you are on vacation; another day you need to work a fifteen-hour shift to solve a major breakdown; another day you are taking an advanced training course. Not all days are the same. So, daily rituals might happen most days, but not every day.

Building rituals is a key rhythm strategy to living a better life. Rituals improve your personal performance and solidify values in your family or team. Across longer cycles, such as a year, rituals become traditions. Across shorter cycles, such as a week, rituals become habits and disciplines. Rituals will give you a more fulfilling life with less burnout and more achievement of what really matters.

---

LIFE EXERCISE: *Identify a life-enhancing ritual that you can build for at least one chronos cycle.*

# 12
# Chronos Strategy #3: Oscillate Work and Rest

*Stress isn't bad. Stress all the time is bad. Downtime isn't a waste of time. Too much downtime is a waste of life.*

MATTHEW KELLY, *THE RHYTHM OF LIFE*

*There is a time for everything, and a season for every activity under heaven:*
*. . . a time to tear down and a time to build,*
*. . . a time to weep and a time to laugh,*
*. . . a time to tear and a time to mend.*

ECCLESIASTES 3:1, 3–4, 7

Roger, my burned-out professor friend, might have avoided burnout if he had practiced oscillation. He ignored his own duty cycles. Life is not a marathon but a series of sprints and rests. If we try to keep a constant pace, we build up higher and higher levels of stress. Humans are not made to do that.

Even man-made machines operate best on duty cycles. We take in our cars for scheduled maintenance (or we know we should). We change the oil about every three months or three thousand miles. In Texas, we change the filters in the air-conditioning units in our homes monthly. Yet we do not adequately consider our own human duty cycles. We, too, need regular rest, renewal, and restoration.

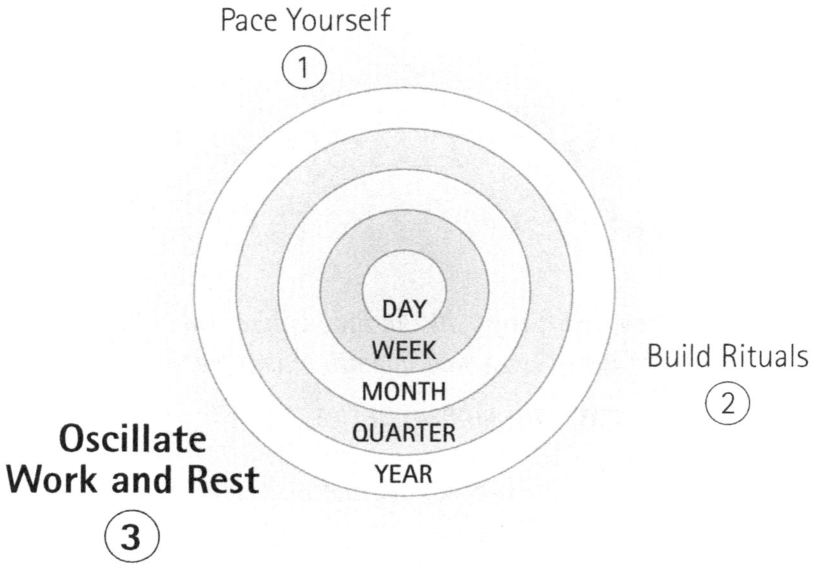


## Jesus Models and Teaches Oscillation

Jesus says to deny ourselves, leave everything behind, and follow him. And yet, while Jesus says to take up our cross, he also says, "Come to me, all you who are weary and burdened, and I will give you rest. Take my yoke upon you and learn from me, for I am gentle and humble in heart, and you will find rest for your souls. For my yoke is easy and my burden is light" (Matthew 11:28-30). *The Message* paraphrase puts it this way:

> Are you tired? Worn out? Burned out on religion? Come to me.
>
> Get away with me and you'll recover your life. I'll show you

> how to take a real rest. Walk with me and work with me—watch
> how I do it. Learn the unforced rhythms of grace. I won't lay
> anything heavy or ill-fitting on you. Keep company with me and
> you'll learn to live freely and lightly.[1]

How can both be true? How can we take up our cross and also take on an easy yoke? We can't if we're trying to stay balanced. But it makes a lot more sense if we understand cross bearing and yoke bearing to be in rhythm over the seasons of our lives.

The Bible calls us to both Sabbath rest and sacrifice. We are to stop working at times, and we are to work sacrificially at other times. We are to set aside time to rest, and we are to take risks for God. We are called to be, at times, both Mary and Martha (see Luke 10:38-42). We sit at Jesus' feet to learn, and we exercise hospitality by "washing feet" to serve (see John 13). The point is not that rest and work are to be kept in balance but that they are to be in rhythm over time. We are to fast and to feast, but not at the same time![2]

Jesus' own life was not balanced, but it was rhythmic. He grew up in his parents' home, then worked as a single man doing carpentry. At thirty years of age, he started a three-year itinerant ministry with a growing circle of followers. During Jesus' ministry, some days he worked long hours. Even when his disciples wanted to send the crowds away, he would not. He told the disciples to feed them (Mark 6:37). Other days, he sent the crowds away so he could be alone on a mountain (Matthew 14:23). At least one

> Jesus' own life was not balanced, but it was rhythmic.

night, he stayed up all night to pray (Luke 6:12). Other times, he rose before the sun to pray (Mark 1:35). Then, when his "hour" came, he lived the last week of his life fully.

Where is the balance? I cannot think of one godly person in the Bible who lived a "balanced" life.[3] Jesus oscillated between times of intensity and times of renewal.

## Oscillation Gives Us "Full Engagement"

The rhythm strategy of oscillation correlates with the insights of Jim Loehr and Tony Schwartz, consultants to world-class athletes and Fortune 500 executives. In their book *The Power of Full Engagement*, they explain the power of oscillation. The process of building muscles serves as an analogy for building our lives.

> Stress is not the enemy in our lives. Paradoxically, it is the key to growth. In order to build strength in a muscle we must systematically stress it, expending energy beyond normal levels. Doing so literally causes microscopic tears in the muscle fibers. At the end of a training session, functional capacity is diminished. But give the muscle twenty-four to forty-eight hours to recover and it grows stronger and better able to handle the next stimulus. . . . This insight both simplifies and revolutionizes the way we approach the barriers that stand in our way.[4]

To grow, we must experience stress. We must push ourselves past normal levels in order to expand our capacity. "To maintain a powerful pulse in our lives, we must learn how to rhythmically spend and renew energy."[5]

What is oscillation? Though the science of physics offers

formal definitions, Loehr and Schwartz provide a practical explanation: "the rhythmic movement between energy expenditure (stress) and energy renewal (recovery)."[6] To relieve stress and increase joy, we aim for optimal cycles of work/rest intervals.

The point is not merely that we need rest, but that we need *both* rest and work, intensity and renewal. "Chronic stress without recovery and chronic recovery without stress both serve to reduce capacity. In sports, these conditions are referred to as overtraining and undertraining."[7] What's the opposite of oscillation? Linearity. "Linearity is excessive stress without recovery or excessive recovery with insufficient stress."[8] That is not a good life. From their observations, Loehr and Schwartz assert, "Most of us are undertrained physically and spiritually (not enough stress) and overtrained mentally and emotionally (not enough recovery)."[9] We need both stress and recovery.

The point is not merely that we need rest, but that we need *both* rest and work.

Psychologist Mihaly Csikszentmihalyi, the author of *Flow*, writes, "The best moments usually occur when a person's body or mind is stretched to its limits in a voluntary effort to accomplish something difficult and worthwhile."[10] Relish these times of intensity when you are competing at the highest level, when you push yourself to your limits. It can be exhilarating. Joy comes from the moments of intensity *and* from the moments of recovery. I've found great joy climbing a mountain, pushing myself to my limit, and I've found great joy lying on a beach, totally relaxed. To reduce stress and increase joy, we need to climb mountains *and* lie on beaches.

Times of intensity need to be matched by times of renewal. Loehr and Schwartz trace the concept of interval training, which is popular today, back to ancient Rome. "The concept of maximizing performance by alternating periods of activity with periods of rest was first advanced by Flavius Philostatus (AD 170–245), who wrote training manuals for Greek athletes." In recent times, "Russian sports scientists resurrected the concept in the 1960s and began applying it with stunning success to their Olympic athletes. Today, 'work-rest' ratios lie at the heart of periodization, a training method used by elite athletes throughout the world."[11]

This oscillating rhythm applies to all of life. "Too much energy expenditure without sufficient recovery eventually leads to burnout and breakdown. (Overuse it and lose it.) Too much recovery without sufficient stress leads to atrophy and weakness. (Use it or lose it.)"[12] We need both kinds of seasons. Whichever season you are in, whether it is one of intensity or one of rest, live it to the fullest. Truly rest when it is time to rest, and be fully intense when it is time to work. A joyful life that achieves its mission requires a dynamic rhythm of moving from expenditure of energy to the renewal of energy in all dimensions of life.

From the realm of music, Matthew Kelly makes a complementary point: "Rests and pauses are as important in great music as the notes themselves. Rests and pauses are as important in great lives as activity."[13] Applying the physical principle to our whole lives, Loehr and Schwartz write,

> The richest, happiest and most productive lives are characterized by the ability to fully engage in the challenge at hand, but also to disengage periodically and seek renewal. Instead, many of us live our lives as if we are running in an endless marathon, pushing ourselves far beyond healthy levels of exertion. We become flat liners

> mentally and emotionally by relentlessly spending energy without sufficient recovery. We become flat liners physically and spiritually by not expending enough energy. Either way, we slowly but inexorably wear down.[14]

We must rhythmically move from engagement to disengagement, from exertion to recovery. If we flatline by neither fully exerting nor fully resting, we wear down and fill our lives with stress or boredom. What we want is not a balance between exertion and recovery, but an oscillation between them.

What we want is not a balance between exertion and recovery, but an oscillation between them.

Weight lifters know how far to push themselves in order to damage muscle tissue just enough so that it rebuilds stronger, but not so far that the athletes injure themselves. Then they wait an adequate time for that muscle to repair itself before they work it again. There is a pattern, a cycle to the process.

The principle of rhythmic oscillation applies in other aspects of life, even those beyond our control. In his work *The Tyranny of Time*, Robert J. Banks points out, "As we oscillate between health and sickness, we should recognize the behavior appropriate to each. Illness needs to be given its time so that we return to full health."[15] I confess that I usually try to push through illness, to keep going even when I know I should stop and realize I'm in a new, hopefully short, season of illness and ought to behave appropriately for that season. If you're sick, get rest. Stop going to the office. Stay home.

Banks describes various kinds of psychological rhythms. He says we should consider times for privacy as well as for enjoying company. "A balance should be struck between large gatherings and smaller ones, between times devoted to strangers and time with friends, between demanding, time-intensive, people-oriented periods and relaxed, time-expansive, self-regarding ones."[16] Even though Banks uses the *b* word—*balance*—he is actually describing rhythmic oscillation from one kind of activity to another over time, not all of them at the same time.

## Applying the Oscillation Strategy in Chronos Cycles

Oscillation can be an abstract concept, but you can make it practical by applying it to the five chronos cycles. Understanding the flow of each cycle, you can now consider how to oscillate between work and rest, exertion and renewal in each one. As you considered life-enhancing rituals in each cycle, now also envision life-renewing oscillation in each cycle.

Oscillation can be an abstract concept, but you can make it practical by applying it to the five chronos cycles.

For each chronos cycle, you can ask yourself this question: *When am I at my best, and when do I need to rest?* Personality factors into the answer. Are you more of an introvert or an extrovert? Does being with people deplete your energy or replenish it? What about being alone? Some people are morning birds and others are night owls. How can you oscillate between work and rest in each cycle?

### OSCILLATION IN ANNUAL CYCLES

As you think through the flow of your annual cycle, consider the ebb and flow of work, the times of intensity and dormancy, high seasons and low seasons. In the course of a year, a farmer has planting times, harvest times, and fallow times.

You will likely experience seasons of intense work to

complete a project, finish a degree, launch a new business, or work a second job. But if you plan rhythmically, you will also live in seasons of rest and re-creation when you slow down. When is the best time of the year for pursuing a major project? When is the best time for a longer vacation?

In my annual cycle, the church world slows down midsummer, so I take a longer break in June or July. Easter and Christmas are intense times, with extra services and special events—not a good time for me to take an extended break. Each September and January, ministries begin a new season of Bible studies and programs for children. We usually launch a new sermon series then, as well. I take time in July to study in advance for the series that will begin in September.

Perhaps in one part of the year, you are going to work seventy or eighty hours a week to launch a new product, but as you look at the whole year, you also know that you are then going to take a two-week vacation. When you finally take the two-week vacation, it would be crazy to feel guilty that you aren't working—but that happens when people are trying to live a life of balance, not realizing that different times call for different rhythms.

During a vacation, you need to really rest, not balance rest with something else. In the opening scene of Arthur Miller's *Death of a Salesman*, there is a famous bedtime dialogue between Willy Loman and his wife, Linda. Willy, an aging salesman, has returned from a business trip, tired and shaken by veering off the road in his car on the way home. A concerned Linda tells Willy he needs to rest. Willy reminds her they have just been on vacation. Linda insightfully asserts, "But

During a vacation, you need to really rest, not balance rest with something else.

you didn't rest your mind. Your mind is overactive, and the mind is what counts, dear."[17]

By learning how to apply the strategy of oscillation in an annual cycle, you can seize opportunities you may have otherwise missed to accomplish something significant, as well as seize opportunities to renew deeply. Because you are achieving a healthy rhythm over the course of a year, the benefits of oscillation may not be evident in any one particular week, but you can relax about the pressure of "imbalance" in a given week because you know that a time of recovery is ahead. By taking a macro view, the oscillations of an annual cycle give perspective to the micro view of the weekly and daily cycles.

Annually, the Dallas Cowboys oscillate between preseason, regular season, play-off season (they hope), and off-season. In the seasons of our lives, some of our stress comes from trying to live either in play-off mode or in off-season mode all the time; or worse yet, from trying to balance both in every season. A better life involves oscillation over the course of the year.

If you are a student, you can maximize your energy using the strategy of oscillation. You should study harder during finals than any other time. You should rest during the breaks so you are ready to come back strong.

Here is where the chronos cycles and the kairos seasons can come together. Years follow upon years with permanent regularity. When you oscillate between work and rest, at each time of the year you seize the opportunity of either intense performance or personal renewal—and you enjoy both, releasing false expectations that you should rest while you are working or work while you are resting.

How can you arrange the flow of your life by anticipating what will come on an annual basis? If you oscillate between times of intensity and times of renewal, you will live a better life, full of more joy, peace, and fulfillment. You will accomplish more with less stress and frustration.

What is your busy season? When is it slow? What is the best time of the year for you to start a large new initiative? When might you want to give extended time in volunteer service or go on a mission trip? When might you engage in further education, such as taking a course or going to a seminar? When could you best run a 10K race or join a volleyball league? Think in advance about how you will stay healthy through the year by oscillating between intensity and renewal.

Think in advance about how you will stay healthy through the year by oscillating between intensity and renewal.

Studies provide compelling evidence that regular vacations improve health. Using results from a heart study, researchers found that women who took a vacation only once every six years were almost eight times more likely to develop heart disease or have a heart attack than those who took at least two vacations a year. A study of twelve thousand men ages thirty-five to fifty-seven by the State University of New York at Oswego found that "men who took yearly vacations reduced their overall risk of death by about 20 percent, and their risk of death from heart disease by as much as 30 percent."[18] According to Dr. Kay Judge and Dr. Maxine Barish-Wreden, various studies indicate that vacations improve marital intimacy, sleep, and mood, as well as decrease physical complaints and fatigue.[19] This strategy applies not only to individuals but also to groups and organizations. If you lead a team, strategize how you will oscillate between work and rest. Perhaps you want to gather your team once a quarter for training or a social experience to build camaraderie.

What yearly oscillations could you strategize in your marriage? with your children? in your relationship with God? with your health? in your home? your school? your community?

Parents ensure that their children are well rested before the school year begins. They don't want their kids to start school tired on the first day. When you are burned out, it is not time to start a new enterprise or major project; it is time to rest and recover. To the extent that your time is in your control, consider what kind of season you need next. Have you been resting and it's now time to get to work, or are you exhausted and it's time to take a vacation? When it is time to work, work hard, excel, push yourself to the limit. When it is time to renew, rest deeply and recover.

To the extent that your time is in your control, consider what kind of season you need next.

## OSCILLATION IN MONTHLY CYCLES

How can you oscillate between times of intensity and times of re-creation on a monthly basis? Is there a time in the month when you are at your best? A time when you need to rest? Based on your responsibilities and context, does the beginning, middle, or end of the month most affect your cycle of work and rest? For moms of little kids, it makes little difference; for car salesmen, it makes a big difference.

Consider all four weekends at one time. Which of them are for work? Which of them are for renewal? Perhaps one weekend you will be out of town at a trade show, conference, or workshop. Perhaps another weekend you will go fishing at the lake. Some weekends should be intense. Perhaps you are painting your house or planting a garden. Depending on how you are wired, those activities could be a depleting time of work or a replenishing time of renewal.

During a month, there should be times to golf, engage in a hobby, goof off, play, and rest. There should be other times to work late to finish a project or handle an emergency. The stress gets out of control when we are always working or always resting. We need to oscillate between both through the cycle of the month.

### OSCILLATION IN WEEKLY CYCLES

In his book *Making Room for Life: Trading Chaotic Lifestyles for Connected Relationships*, Randy Frazee recommends what he calls "the Hebrew Day Planner," an ancient concept new to most people in our day. He writes, "The basic premise of the Hebrew Day Planner is that we were designed by God on the sixth day of creation to function in harmony and rhythm with what he created on the first five days."[20] One implication is to take one day a week to rest and replenish.

Some years ago, I worked seven days a week on a regular basis. I did not put in a full day on Saturday, but the rest of the days were fairly heavy. My rationale was that I was starting a new church and so much had to happen. Of course, I worked on Sundays—some people thought that was the only day I worked because that was when they heard me speak!

One year, late in the fall, the elders, the governing board of the church, strongly encouraged me to take a day off. Basically, it was a directive. I'm sure they were worried that I would burn out. I countered, "Don't take a day away from me; if anything, add a day." After some consideration, by faith, I agreed that at the start of the new year I would take off every Friday for three months and then evaluate how it was going.

*I will never go back to working seven days a week*. Frankly, I was amazed that by taking one day each week to rest, I actually got more done in the other six days than I was getting done in seven days before. Every day of the week, I was more refreshed and sharper because I took time to rest and recuperate on Fridays. That is the power of oscillation in chronos cycles to free you from burnout.

By taking one day each week to rest, I actually got more done in the other six days than I was getting done in seven days before.

In the cycle of your week, ask yourself, *When am I at my best, and when do I need to rest?* Is there a day of the week where your energy is at its highest? Tackle the toughest or most important stuff that day. Solve the most complicated problems. Then, when can you best rest? What day will you take off—meaning take time to renew, to do whatever replenishes your energy?

For me, I schedule team meetings on Mondays, research sermons on Tuesdays, commit my talk to manuscript on Wednesdays, meet with individuals on Thursdays, and take off Fridays and Saturdays. Sundays, of course, are taken up with church services. My best weekly time for longer-range thinking and brainstorming meetings is Thursday mornings.

### OSCILLATION IN DAILY CYCLES

To oscillate daily, focus on discretionary time. In the cycle of most days, do you have more discretionary time in the morning or in the evening? Most people are required to work during the day. How will you oscillate in the hours over which you have the most discretion? Each week has seven days, offering you seven mornings and seven evenings. If you have a free lunch hour, how will you use those seven lunchtimes?

The day is formed by the oscillation of day and night, light and dark. We are designed to rest at night and work in the daylight. But the invention of the lightbulb gave us the means to break that cycle, and in doing so we have hurt ourselves.

Take time to think through the best flow of an ideal day for you, realizing that no day is "typical." When would you wake up, and when would you go to sleep? When would you tackle your most difficult jobs? When would you renew yourself on a daily basis?

Studies consistently show that lack of sleep slows reaction time, decreases concentration, degrades memory, and directly leads to a steady decline in logical reasoning. The average human body needs seven or eight hours of sleep per twenty-four-hour period. Six or less hours triples your risk of a car accident (not enough renewal), but more than nine hours can also harm your health (not enough work). We heal and grow during sleep, which is one of our most important times of recovery. If you are not sleeping well, you will increase your stress and reduce your joy, as well as that of the people around you, because sleep deprivation drives grouchiness. Sleep is a daily oscillation for renewal.

Lack of sleep slows reaction time, decreases concentration, degrades memory, and directly leads to a steady decline in logical reasoning.

Not only does sleep overcome serious negatives, but it also replenishes us with positive energy. According to a report in the *Dallas Morning News*, Dr. Nilesh Dave, medical director of the Sleep and Breathing Disorders Center at the University of Texas Southwestern Medical Center, shared five benefits of getting adequate sleep. Getting good sleep makes us better athletes, helps us deal with stress, helps us remember, is imperative for safe driving, and keeps us from being crabby.[21]

It is widely known that sleep occurs in cycles of 90 to 120 minutes. Newer research on naps reveals what many famous high achievers already know intuitively—that similar 90- to 120-minute cycles called ultradian rhythms operate in our waking lives as well. These cycles help explain the ebb and flow of our energy throughout the day. The human body craves oscillation. You stifle a yawn, stretch, feel hungry, have a hard time concentrating, begin to daydream, make more mistakes—all signs of ebbing energy, and totally normal. It is best to work hard for ninety minutes, then take a short break and go back for another ninety-minute focus period.

The attempt to maintain linearity is unnatural and harmful physically, emotionally, mentally, and spiritually.

The power of living in rhythm is to flow with the natural cycles of our bodies and our world. When we try to fight the cycles with stimulants such as coffee, energy drinks, or amphetamines, we damage ourselves over the long term. Then, when we can't relax, we turn to alcohol, marijuana, or sleeping pills. The attempt to maintain linearity is unnatural and harmful physically, emotionally, mentally, and spiritually.

The National Institute of Mental Health authorized a release affirming that "power naps" prevent burnout.[22] Sara Mednick, who is at the forefront of napping research, says, "Napping maintains and even boosts your skills, from creative problem solving and alertness and physical stamina, to mood and memory."[23]

However, too much napping can make you drowsier. When you wake up from a nap, have you had the experience where your limbs feel like concrete, your eyes can't focus, you slur your speech, and your mind is in low gear? Generally, naps that last more than twenty minutes can create sleep inertia.[24]

Fighting natural cycles makes us crazy. Living in tune with

created cycles brings harmony to our lives. Oscillate between work and rest in the chronos cycles to increase your joy. For high performance, choose times to work long hours and many consecutive days; identify your best times of the week and the day for accomplishing difficult tasks. For renewal, take an annual vacation; take a weekend each month for downtime; take a day off weekly; and get good sleep daily. Climb mountains, and relax on beaches. Work hard and play well.

Following the three rhythm strategies in the chronos cycles—pace yourself, build life-enhancing rituals, and oscillate between work and rest—will give you a better life. Through pace, rituals, and oscillation, you will decrease guilt, burnout, and stress while increasing peace, fulfillment, and hope. Adding to these strategies the three kairos rhythm strategies—release expectations, seize opportunities, and anticipate what's next—will further enhance your life.

We were made for more than just this short life span. However, we can experience a better life on earth if we will apply the six rhythm strategies. When you live in rhythm, you accomplish more, more peacefully. Using a Rhythm Solution Process can help you put the strategies into practice.

---

LIFE EXERCISE: *Identify an oscillation between work and rest that you can introduce in at least one chronos cycle.*

PART IV

# A Rhythm Solution Process

13

# Putting It All Together

*Rhythm is something you either have or don't have, but when you have it, you have it all over.*

ELVIS PRESLEY

The goal is to have a better life, a life characterized by less stress, more peace, less burnout, more fulfillment, and less discouragement with more hope. How can you put all six rhythm strategies together to make them work for you?

Start with your real-life situation. Describe a problem or struggle in your life. You might recall the issues you identified at the end of chapter 2. Then use a Rhythm Solution Process worksheet (see appendix B) to put the rhythm strategies to work solving your problem.

## Define the Problem

It is worth taking time to really understand the problem. Economist Henry Hazlitt writes, "A problem properly stated is a problem partly solved."[1] Problem solving begins with a mess, an ill-defined challenge, a confusing tangle of feelings and data. Often we race to solutions before we have honestly grasped the problem we are attempting to solve. It's foolish to answer a question we do not really understand, but we try anyway.

In marriage, it is typical for a husband to start solving a problem before his wife has even finished explaining the situation. If you have not already discovered it, this approach usually leads to disaster, especially when a husband addresses what he thinks is his wife's issue, but he is dead wrong. Time taken at the front end to grasp the issue is directly proportional to time needed at the back end to solve the issue. When you go off in a wrong direction at the start, you inevitably waste time correcting your mistake in the end.

Operating from a balance paradigm often leads to a faulty assessment of the problems in your life. For example, Mike Jones thought his problem was an issue of balancing all the demands in his life. He assumed that he needed to manage his time better and somehow find the mirage of a perfectly balanced arrangement of responsibilities. Actually, Mike was trying to live in too many rhythms at the same time. He was importing expectations that did not fit his current life stage or his personal season. Manifestations of his situation included high levels of stress and a floating sense of anxiety because he wasn't doing all he was supposed to do in any arena of his life. Ironically, the more he pressed toward the balance mirage, the worse he felt.

Using the Rhythm Solution Process to sort out situations also helps in diagnosing the deeper issues underneath the surface symptoms.

I find that using the Rhythm Solution Process to sort out situations also helps in diagnosing the deeper issues underneath the surface symptoms. One suburban family doctor said that more than half the people he treats suffer from stress-related health problems. Addressing deeper issues relieves chronic worry, which, when alleviated, frequently heals the physical health problems created by the stress.

## Review Your Foundations for Intentional Living

Are you living intentionally? Do you have a life mission that you can articulate? Do you know why you are alive and what you are hoping to do with your life? If you have never worked through the process of writing a life mission statement, I encourage you to complete that exercise as part of the process of bringing your life into rhythm. (For more information about life mission, go to www.yourlifeinrhythm.com.)

Next, you need to be aware of all your stewardships, those things for which you are responsible. Core stewardships include being an employee, a parent, and a member of the community. (For more information about life stewardships, go to www.yourlifeinrhythm.com.)

With these directional pieces in place, you can make wise decisions in regard to the rhythms of your life because you have answered the foundational question of mission (Where are you going?) and stewardship (For whom and for what are you responsible?). These are two keys to living intentionally.

## Apply the Rhythm Solution Process

The Rhythm Solution Process serves as a tool to help you think through how one or more of the six rhythm strategies could help you in your current situation. Use the rhythm strategies that best address your issue. The process gives you a track to run on, a way to quickly and easily see how to think rhythmically about a life issue. You can apply all the strategies, but most of the time, using just a few will give you the most help.

### IDENTIFY WHAT TIME IT IS

After describing the problem, the first step in the solution process is to identify what time it is in your life. What personal seasons are you experiencing, and in what life stage are you? Are your stresses related more to a personal season or your life stage—or both?

### APPLY THE KAIROS RHYTHM STRATEGIES

Focusing on the season or stage that is creating the most challenge, ask yourself, "What *expectations* can I release to increase my peace? What *opportunities* can I seize to increase my joyful fulfillment? What can I *anticipate* to increase my hope?" Then move to the chronos strategies.

### APPLY THE CHRONOS RHYTHM STRATEGIES

*Pace yourself:* Can you reset the frequency of some activities? Can you create a better flow within a cycle?

*Build rituals:* What life-enhancing traditions can you set in longer cycles? What life-enhancing habits can you establish in shorter cycles?

*Oscillate between work and rest:* Do you need more work or more rest right now? How can you oscillate better in one or more of the five chronos cycles?

### INVOLVE ANOTHER PERSON

None of us see ourselves clearly. When your problems are long-standing, complex, or just really difficult for you to solve, involve a trusted friend or wise adviser to help. Often, another person can quickly see something you can't see because you are too close to it. We all have blind spots and default tendencies. For instance, you might be the kind of person whose default is to work hard. You are more likely to feel the need to be in a rhythm of intensity. Other people may most often believe it is time to rest. What they think they need is a vacation. Stress can confuse us. Rest is not always the best cure for stress. Sometimes, rather than napping in your recliner in front of the TV, you can better reduce your stress by jogging on the treadmill at the gym or by gutting it out to finish the project hanging over your head. A trusted friend who knows you can often give you more objective input than you can give yourself.

> When your problems are long-standing, complex, or just really difficult for you to solve, involve a trusted friend or wise adviser to help.

A friend can also provide you with accountability. The infamous road to hell is proverbially paved with good intentions. As valuable as it will be for you to work through the Rhythm Solution Process, if you only write down action steps on paper, you will not make changes in your life. Diets are effective only to the extent they are actually followed. If you will share your rhythm solutions with a friend, he or she can hold you accountable. Ask your friend to follow up with you in a few weeks. Invite him or her to ask you how you are doing. Just the act of sharing your plan with another person will improve your follow-through.

## Case Studies

Let's work through a few real-life situations, case studies of how you can apply the six rhythm strategies. I've selected a variety of people. In each case, I briefly describe the problem. Then, the first step in every person's situation is to consider what time it is in his or her life. In what personal seasons and life stage is he or she living?

At that point, I look over the kairos and chronos rhythm strategies to see which one (or ones) would offer the most help. Usually, one to three strategies directly address a given problem. It is possible to apply all six strategies to each person's situation, but that is usually overkill. Most people can take only one or two action steps at any given time. Even when I recommend a solution that involves multiple steps, I will suggest that a person start with just one or two of the most powerful steps and then move to the next ones.

The act of sharing your plan with another person will improve your follow-through.

Following the case studies, you will find a blank worksheet you can use to develop a solution for an issue in your life. There are more worksheets available for download from www.yourlifeinrhythm.com. Feel free to copy them.

# Rhythm Solution Process

NAME: *Chris, a single college graduate*

*Chris, who has a degree in communications, wants to break into sports radio. He is working all-night shifts at a top station, earning low pay working as an intern. To get health benefits, he also works part-time at Starbucks, pulling shifts at all hours of the day. He is chronically exhausted and feels like a failure. On top of his two jobs, he volunteers with a junior high program at church and leads worship in a young adult ministry. He lives in the same town with his family, with whom he is quite close. He said he is tired of hanging up his apron next to his college diploma.*

| | |
|---|---|
| Identify the Problem | *Chris is missing the opportunities of this life stage and holding on to false expectations.* |
| Identify Personal Seasons and Life Stages | PERSONAL SEASONS: *Recently, Chris went through a difficult breakup with his girlfriend, who quickly got engaged to her ex-boyfriend; providing game-day analysis at the radio station for Dallas Cowboys games.*<br><br>LIFE STAGE: *Young, single, just out of college, getting started in a career* |
| Apply Kairos Rhythm Strategies | RELEASE EXPECTATIONS: *With the intensity of work needed to start a career and dealing with the pain of a breakup, it's not a good time for a girlfriend; release the expectation of a serious dating relationship. As an intern in the sports-radio business, financial reward takes longer to realize than in some other occupations; release the expectation of higher compensation compared to fellow college graduates in other fields. Also release the expectation that you can volunteer in two large roles in your church during this time.* |
| | SEIZE OPPORTUNITIES: *Learn all you can at one of the top stations in the nation, working with national sports-radio personalities. Enjoy meeting top athletes and coaches. Go to whatever games you can using free tickets.* |
| | ANTICIPATE WHAT'S NEXT: *You will not be an intern forever. On the horizon, within a few years you will likely have a full-time job and a girlfriend, maybe even a wife. Look forward to those things in their time.* |
| Apply Chronos Rhythm Strategies | SET YOUR PACE (FREQUENCY AND FLOW): *Commit to Thursday Bible study in lieu of church attendance on Sundays because of all-night Saturday shifts and early football games on Sunday.* |
| | BUILD RITUALS (TRADITIONS AND HABITS): *Because family is important, set a weekly ritual to spend time at your parents' house with your younger brother. (This is also an opportunity to seize, because you are living in the same town.)* |
| | OSCILLATE BETWEEN WORK AND REST: *Negotiate with the radio station and Starbucks so you are not working days and nights that run together the same week. Every few months (quarterly), take off for a few days. Go visit friends; get out of town.* |

# Rhythm Solution Process

NAME: *Mary, a stressed-out college student*

*Mary, in the midst of her toughest semester of college, is a highly stressed college student. On top of eighteen credit hours, there are labs and rehearsals for her music major. An important scholarship rides on keeping good grades.*

| | |
|---|---|
| **Identify the Problem** | *Mary is trying to live this semester just as she did other ones.* |
| **Identify Personal Seasons and Life Stages** | PERSONAL SEASONS: *Toughest semester; boyfriend just entered same college; her sorority is preparing for January rush*<br><br>LIFE STAGE: *College student* |
| **Apply Kairos Rhythm Strategies** | RELEASE EXPECTATIONS: *Release the expectation of working a job this semester, so expect to have less money. Tell your boyfriend you will not be able see each other as much this semester, releasing this relationship's time expectation. Release the expectation of going home as many weekends as you did in previous semesters, and inform your parents of your reasons.* |
| | SEIZE OPPORTUNITIES: *Learn from all your classes; this is the time for education. Participate fully in vocal competitions; enjoy sorority activities.* |
| | ANTICIPATE WHAT'S NEXT: *Next semester will be easier, with fewer hours; Christmas break is coming soon.* |
| **Apply Chronos Rhythm Strategies** | SET YOUR PACE (FREQUENCY AND FLOW): *Set a weekly study schedule around classes and sorority obligations.* |
| | BUILD RITUALS (TRADITIONS AND HABITS): |
| | OSCILLATE BETWEEN WORK AND REST: *Study hard. This is your semester to press hard in school. Weekly, stop studying and do something to relax and unwind. Go to the marshmallow cookout on Saturday nights. Quarterly, rest well during school breaks. Take a long weekend to go on a road trip. Go home and crash.* |

# Rhythm Solution Process

NAME: *Lu, a new mom*

*A recent immigrant from Mexico, Lu is a high-energy person who has always worked hard, often taking courses while working a full-time job and volunteering on top of that. She just had her first baby (a boy), and life as she knew it has come to a screeching halt. She feels very ill at ease. She had planned to go back to work, but now it doesn't seem practical. She can't exercise or volunteer as she had been doing.*

| | |
|---|---|
| **Identify the Problem** | *Lu is not embracing her new stage of life.* |
| **Identify Personal Seasons and Life Stages** | PERSONAL SEASONS: *Mother of a newborn baby boy*<br><br>LIFE STAGE: *Young mother with first child* |
| **Apply Kairos Rhythm Strategies** | RELEASE EXPECTATIONS: *Release the expectation of going to the office to work; release expectations of attending school and volunteering long hours.* |
| | SEIZE OPPORTUNITIES: *This is your time to raise your little boy. Love him and cherish every moment with him. Enjoy working reduced hours at home on the new laptop from the company.* |
| | ANTICIPATE WHAT'S NEXT: *In five or six years, your boy will be in school, at least half days. In eighteen years, your baby will be leaving home.* |
| **Apply Chronos Rhythm Strategies** | *In Lu's case, we employ only kairos strategies, because that is the main need. We could also talk about a new pace and building life-enhancing rituals with a new baby, but those can wait for another day. You can read more of Lu's story on the Web site: www.yourlifeinrhythm.com.* |

# Rhythm Solution Process

NAME: *Darrell and Tonya, retired and in a crisis*

*In their retirement years, Darrell and Tonya are unexpectedly facing a major crisis that is creating huge stress, resulting in physical and emotional health issues. Their adult daughter was in the midst of building a log home on acreage when she was divorced and lost her job as an executive. She is depressed and now is about to lose both the half-built home and the land to the bank. There is tension with the builder. Darrell and Tonya have stepped in to help, assuming the loan, hiring a new builder, and managing the project. All their time is consumed with working and worrying. They are not sleeping at night.*

| | |
|---|---|
| **Identify the Problem** | *Darrell and Tonya have conflicting expectations in conflicting rhythms* |
| **Identify Personal Seasons and Life Stages** | PERSONAL SEASONS: *Dealing with an adult daughter who is divorced, unemployed, and stuck with a loan on a house and property*<br><br>LIFE STAGE: *Retired* |
| **Apply Kairos Rhythm Strategies** | RELEASE EXPECTATIONS: *One option could have been to release the expectation that you need to rescue your adult daughter and allow her to let the property go. However, because you have assumed the mortgage and have taken on this large and urgent project, release previous retirement expectations of the same level of financial security, volunteer responsibilities, and financial support of missionaries. Take a leave of absence from giving time and money to causes you believe in.* |
| | SEIZE OPPORTUNITIES: *Invest in your daughter, helping her to recover. You may never have another opportunity to spend this much time with your adult daughter.* |
| | ANTICIPATE WHAT'S NEXT: *Your daughter will get back on her feet and may move into the log house or to a new place. This season will pass. You will get back to your retirement life.* |
| **Apply Chronos Rhythm Strategies** | SET YOUR PACE (FREQUENCY AND FLOW): *Choose a period of time each day to spend on resolving the situation with your daughter; then let it go for the rest of the day.* |
| | BUILD RITUALS (TRADITIONS AND HABITS): *Exercise daily for stress relief and for the health benefits; walk together around the lake after lunch.* |
| | OSCILLATE BETWEEN WORK AND REST: *Work hard to do what needs to be done in this brief season of intensity.* |

# Rhythm Solution Process

NAME: *Bill and Susan, a couple whose fifteen-year marriage is in trouble*

*In their own words, "Our marriage is a mess. Past bad decisions have ruined trust between us. We don't even like each other anymore. Life is so crazy that we never have time to really talk."*

| | |
|---|---|
| Identify the Problem | *Bill and Susan are growing further apart.* |
| Identify Personal Seasons and Life Stages | PERSONAL SEASONS: *Bill has been offered a major promotion with new responsibilities, including travel. It is the middle of their kids' school year.*<br>LIFE STAGE: *Midlife, married, raising kids who are just hitting teenage years* |
| Apply Kairos Rhythm Strategies | RELEASE EXPECTATIONS: *An evaluation of life mission and stewardships can determine if this is the time for Bill to accept the promotion. One solution is to turn down the promotion for the sake of their marriage. Susan needs to release unrealistic expectations of Bill that she has because of her dad, who never traveled and was home every day by 5 p.m. Release expectations that you can change the past or repair the effects of the past quickly.* |
| | SEIZE OPPORTUNITIES: *Enjoy the kids' activities together; use some of the increased income from Bill's promotion, if he takes it, for marital counseling sessions.* |
| | ANTICIPATE WHAT'S NEXT: *An empty nest is coming within ten years, so be motivated to work on your marriage because you want a good relationship when there is just the two of you at home.* |
| Apply Chronos Rhythm Strategies | SET YOUR PACE (FREQUENCY AND FLOW): |
| | BUILD RITUALS (TRADITIONS AND HABITS): *Drive together to kids' activities and use the time in the car and waiting at various events to talk; schedule time once a week for a date together; this Friday, go to the Impressionist art exhibit downtown; use frequent-flier miles from Bill's travels to fly somewhere for your anniversary.* |
| | OSCILLATE BETWEEN WORK AND REST: |

# Rhythm Solution Process

NAME: *Michael, a corporate manager overwhelmed with the pressures of business*

*The corporation is demanding more and more time, so Michael is overwhelmed with the pressures of business. All of his time is consumed with work, so he is too exhausted for anything else, including family, friends, and fun. His ex-wife has custody of the kids, but Michael often cannot take his allotted time with the kids because of conflicts with work.*

| | |
|---|---|
| Identify the Problem | *Michael has competing priorities and responsibilities.* |
| Identify Personal Seasons and Life Stages | PERSONAL SEASONS: *Time of rapid growth in the company, where he's rising through the ranks.*<br><br>LIFE STAGE: *Mid-career, divorced father of school-age kids* |
| Apply Kairos Rhythm Strategies | RELEASE EXPECTATIONS: *Revisit your life mission and consider releasing the expectation of rapid promotion; discuss realistic expectations with your boss. Resign from volunteering on a committee in your industry.* |
| | SEIZE OPPORTUNITIES: *Take every possible occasion to be with your kids. Let your boss know this is your priority for their few remaining growing-up years.* |
| | ANTICIPATE WHAT'S NEXT: |
| Apply Chronos Rhythm Strategies | SET YOUR PACE (FREQUENCY AND FLOW): *Address business work flow: what can you delegate, delay, or dispense with? Stop the constant pace. Analyze the rhythm of your business in each of the chronos cycles. At home, develop a kid calendar for each chronos cycle, based on when you have time to be with your kids. Make it as firm as your business commitments. At work, merge the kid calendar with your business calendar, making it visible to coworkers to avoid as many schedule conflicts as possible.* |
| | BUILD RITUALS (TRADITIONS AND HABITS): *Send a daily text to each kid before you start your day. Make a phone call to each kid on Sunday afternoon.* |
| | OSCILLATE BETWEEN WORK AND REST: *Identify how you can oscillate between work and rest in the rhythms of your business, rather than constantly working as hard and as long as you can. Schedule regular downtime to renew yourself. Go to a jazz club on Saturday nights when you don't have the kids.* |

# Rhythm Solution Process

NAME: *Monica, a divorced, single mom with preteen kids*

*Monica says, "My ex is not paying his child support, and we are in court again over ridiculous issues. I'm working one full-time and two part-time jobs to make ends meet. I'm dating. Life is crazy."*

| | |
|---|---|
| **Identify the Problem** | *Monica is having financial issues from the divorce.* |
| **Identify Personal Seasons and Life Stages** | PERSONAL SEASONS: *Divorced, single mom; school year has started; in a legal battle with ex-husband*<br><br>LIFE STAGE: *Midthirties, parenting preteens* |
| **Apply Kairos Rhythm Strategies** | RELEASE EXPECTATIONS: *Because your kids are your priority, release high expectations of dating. Quit one of the part-time jobs and live on less income. Release yourself from the false expectation that you should volunteer as heavily as some moms can.* |
| | SEIZE OPPORTUNITIES: *Invest yourself in your kids; fully engage with them. Enjoy time to yourself without a husband or boyfriend.* |
| | ANTICIPATE WHAT'S NEXT: *Kids will grow up, and you may get remarried. You will have time for more work later, if needed.* |
| **Apply Chronos Rhythm Strategies** | SET YOUR PACE (FREQUENCY AND FLOW): *Automate as many routine tasks as possible; do chores with the kids on a predictable schedule.* |
| | BUILD RITUALS (TRADITIONS AND HABITS): *Create traditions for the kids around birthdays and holidays, but not necessarily on the exact day; that way you can be consistent even when they are with their dad for the holidays.* |
| | OSCILLATE BETWEEN WORK AND REST: *Create rest rhythms in the chronos cycles: Daily, have morning quiet time—sometimes on the porch. Weekly, take Sunday nights off—no activities, everyone stays home. Monthly, take off an entire Saturday for something fun with the kids. Quarterly, take a day for yourself away from the kids. Annually, take a low-budget vacation with the kids (e.g., camping, visiting grandparents).* |

# Rhythm Solution Process

NAME: *Jack, married, with two kids, finishing his MBA*

*Jack never stops between work, studying for his MBA, and helping to care for his two children, ages nine months and two and a half. He feels off balance because he has lost almost all his personal time for friends and sports. His stress level is rising to unhealthy levels, and he is snapping at his wife and kids. He hates losing his temper and feels terribly guilty.*

| | |
|---|---|
| Identify the Problem | *Jack is overcommitted and stressed.* |
| Identify Personal Seasons and Life Stages | PERSONAL SEASONS: *Working on a master's degree*<br><br>LIFE STAGE: *Late twenties, married, parenting young kids* |
| Apply Kairos Rhythm Strategies | RELEASE EXPECTATIONS: *Release the expectation of playing on a softball team this season. During the semester, release the expectation of having much personal time beyond studying for the MBA. Work with your wife to release "honey do" expectations* |
| | SEIZE OPPORTUNITIES: *Learn. That's why you are working toward the MBA. Don't shortcut it. Use drive time to the university to maximize phone calls to clients or take public transportation and use the downtime to nap or listen to your favorite music and chill out.* |
| | ANTICIPATE WHAT'S NEXT: *Graduation! You can do this awhile longer. There is an end in sight. The babies will grow up. You will not change their diapers, feed them, and dress them forever.* |
| Apply Chronos Rhythm Strategies | SET YOUR PACE (FREQUENCY AND FLOW): *A small part of the daily cycle is most important to your wife and kids, so maximize the crucial window from 6 p.m. to 8 p.m. for feeding, baths, and bedtime. Reserve that time for your family, and then study after they go to bed.* |
| | BUILD RITUALS (TRADITIONS AND HABITS): *Read your kids a bedtime story and tuck them in.* |
| | OSCILLATE BETWEEN WORK AND REST: *Plan for downtime during every school break. Play disc golf, go to the lake with your family, sleep late.* |

# Rhythm Solution Process Worksheet

YOUR NAME: ____________________

<table>
<tr><td>Identify the Problem</td><td></td></tr>
<tr><td>Identify Personal Seasons and Life Stages</td><td>PERSONAL SEASONS:<br><br>LIFE STAGE:</td></tr>
<tr><td rowspan="3">Apply Kairos Rhythm Strategies</td><td>RELEASE EXPECTATIONS:</td></tr>
<tr><td>SEIZE OPPORTUNITIES:</td></tr>
<tr><td>ANTICIPATE WHAT'S NEXT:</td></tr>
<tr><td rowspan="3">Apply Chronos Rhythm Strategies</td><td>SET YOUR PACE (FREQUENCY AND FLOW):</td></tr>
<tr><td>BUILD RITUALS (TRADITIONS AND HABITS):</td></tr>
<tr><td>OSCILLATE BETWEEN WORK AND REST:</td></tr>
</table>

## PART V

# Ultimate Rhythm

# 14
# Seeing from Eternity

*He has also set eternity in the hearts of men.*

ECCLESIASTES 3:11

Though living rhythmically will give you a better life, it will not relieve all your struggles or turn everything rosy. We live in a difficult, painful world. Really bad things happen frequently, from cancer to job losses. This side of eternity, life will not be easy. Recognizing the reality of personal and global suffering can be overwhelming. It can lead to despair and hopelessness. But there is an ultimate hope.

So far, we have focused on earthly rhythms. Chronos cycles are generated largely by the movement and location of the Earth, moon, and sun. Kairos seasons happen in the course of human life like waves on the sea. Theologians might associate chronos rhythms with creation and kairos rhythms with providence. But there is another rhythm, an ultimate rhythm. Deep inside, we know this life is not all there is. Nearly every culture has a version of the afterlife. Our art, poetry, and music echo with longings for eternity—the seventh rhythm strategy.

Burnout comes not just from excessive time on life's treadmill but also from the weariness of worrying about the ultimate meaning and purpose of our lives. Is what we are doing really going to matter in the end? What difference will it make when life is over whether I tried to live my life in balance, in rhythm, or in no particular way at all? Seeing from eternity gives a life-changing perspective.

## Meaningful or Meaningless—We Are Made for More

In the ancient Jewish book of Ecclesiastes, King Solomon asks some hard questions about the apparent meaninglessness of life. As a powerful king, he had the resources to try every version of the good life. His experiments yielded few positive results, whether he tried building projects, sexual adventure, endless recreation, or wielding his royal power. He acknowledges that in the end, death still comes to all of us, and memory of us on this earth fades rapidly.

The prospect of eternity gives us the hope of ultimate meaning beyond our short lives.

Yet the prospect of eternity gives us the hope of ultimate meaning beyond our short lives. In Ecclesiastes 3:11, right after his poem on the rhythmic nature of life, Solomon says,

*He has made everything beautiful in its time.*
*He has also set eternity in the hearts of men;*

*yet they cannot fathom what God has done from beginning to end.*

"The point is ironic," writes Bible scholar Choon-Leong Seow. "God who has made everything right in its time has also put a sense of timelessness in human hearts." In Hebrew, the word for *eternity*–that which transcends time–refers to a sense of timelessness, and as such, stands in contrast to "its time," which refers to timeliness.[1]

An inner sense, deep in our hearts, tells us that we are made for more than this brief passing on earth. We instinctively know that this life is not all there is. Though every major civilization has a concept of an afterlife, the Hebrews have one of the most ancient, long-standing traditions. According to Old Testament commentator Michael Eaton,

> "Eternity" was important in Israel's heritage. An eternal life had been lost (Genesis 3:22), and "eternal covenant" inaugurated (Genesis 9:16) by an eternal God (Psalm 90:2). An eternal priesthood (Exodus 40:15) and an eternal kingdom (2 Samuel 7:13) were bestowed by a God eternally merciful (Psalm 111:4-5), giving his people eternal joy (Isaiah 35:10). The eternity of God's dealings with mankind corresponds to something inside us; we have a capacity for eternal things, are concerned about the future, want to understand "from the beginning to the end," and have a sense of something which transcends our immediate situation.[2]

Our rituals of death and our prayers of mourning point to the reality of something that transcends our earthly existence. Even our dreams speak of a life beyond this one.

## Designed for Immortality

It all goes back to the Garden of Eden. We were made conditionally immortal, capable of living forever. But humanity disobeyed God and was cursed with death. Death is not natural to us, even though it is universal. We were created without death, designed to live indefinitely; but that was lost in the Fall. Our original immortality is one reason why death is so deeply sad. Death is an unwelcome, unwanted intruder in our world. It is fundamentally off-key.

When Solomon surveyed the sources of happiness on earth, he ultimately found nothing temporal that fully satisfies the human heart. Saint Augustine said, "You have made us for yourself, and our hearts are restless until they can find peace in you."[3] In *The Tyranny of Time*, Robert J. Banks describes our world as "provisional."[4] Our accomplishments and experiences are always incomplete. He says this phenomenon indicates our genuine longing for the life beyond.

Presuming there is a hereafter, how does that fact affect our lives today? Each of us will face God one day to answer for how we fulfilled our mission, the one for which he placed us on earth (see Romans 14:12). Eternity makes our life mission all the more important; it's crucial to get the mission right, and crucial to carry it out well. The prospect of eternity adds fuel to the significance of our mission here on earth.

> The prospect of eternity adds fuel to the significance of our mission here on earth.

What can we do in this life that we cannot do in eternity? Though the question is not fully answerable because we do not know enough about eternity, we do know that once we leave the earth, we cannot continue to influence other people in the same way we do now. Once we die, it is too late to tell our families that we love them, too late for apologies and reconciliations. It is only in this life that we have those opportunities. The certainty of life's brevity makes those actions so much more crucial and urgent.

The ultimate rhythm of eternity motivates me to be a good steward of all that has been entrusted to me, knowing that God will reward me in eternity based on how I have managed what he has entrusted to me on earth. Jesus asked a telling question at the end of his parable of the shrewd manager: "If you have not been trustworthy in handling worldly wealth, who will trust you with true riches?" (Luke 16:11).

In some ways, our life on the earth is a test—a test of faithfulness. Our fleeting time in this life is merely a dot on the time line of eternity, yet we have the opportunity to influence eternity by how we steward what God entrusts to us today.

## What Can We Do with Our Guilt?

We experience some unnecessary guilt from our false expectations, but other guilty feelings arise from our conscience, which alerts us when we have done something wrong. How can we deal with that kind of guilt? The specter of divine judgment can weigh on our souls and weigh down our lives.

Facing the fact that God is our eternal judge can increase the intensity of our guilt. How will we fare before the holy Judge of all? Our conscience tells us we do not meet our own standards, much less his. And we are right. That guilt is true guilt. No human being has lived a perfect life. So how should we deal with our real guilt?

We can't. Our inability to solve our guilt is a big problem. Only God can deal with our guilt. That's why Jesus Christ died on the cross, to take on our guilt. The Bible says, "God made him who had no sin to be sin for us, so that in him we might become the righteousness of God" (2 Corinthians 5:21). The way to find freedom from true guilt is to avail ourselves of God's forgiveness. Only God can forgive sin. He offers to take away our guilt through Jesus Christ. That is achieving freedom from guilt!

Our inability to solve our guilt is a big problem. Only God can deal with our guilt.

## How Can Seeing from Eternity Reduce Busyness, Stress, and Burnout?

Consider how eternity connects with the rhythms of this life. God created the chronos cycles, but there is no sure indication that these will continue into eternity. Kairos seasons are generated by human life on this fallen planet. And yet, in eternity our life span has no end, our seasons will not be tainted by pain, and we will be in paradise. One day, the eternal *aeon* (age) will overtake *chronos* and *kairos*. We will experience different cycles and have different kairos opportunities in the eternal *aeon*.

So how can an understanding of eternity help us live well today? When you realize both the brevity of this life and the length of the next life, you want to make this life count for forever. It leads you to ask, As seen from heaven, what will matter on earth? Seen from eternity, what will matter in time? What matters most is what will last.

So what will last into eternity? What in this life makes an eternal difference? People. People last eternally. When you are overly busy with so many things, ask yourself which of those things will truly matter in a week? in a year? in eternity? That final, very long-term context helps you sort through your busyness to decide what really matters eternally. What will God care about when you stand before him one day?

These questions help us to avoid burnout, because when we can reduce busyness, we diminish the danger of burning out. More fundamentally, when we focus our lives on what matters forever, we find new meaning and motivation for our lives today. Burnout accelerates when what we are doing seems meaningless. When we lose motivation, life is dreary and depressing. Knowing that what we are doing matters to God for all eternity enables us to continue strong. That knowledge fills us with joy.

> What will last into eternity? What in this life makes an eternal difference? What will God care about when you stand before him one day?

Ordinary tasks, such as washing dishes or filling out expense reports, can wear us out unless we can re-envision them in light of eternity. As we fulfill our responsibilities, we serve other people and bring honor to God, both of which matter for eternity.

However, even with high motivation, life can be difficult and wear us down. Having the assurance that eternity is coming increases our strength to persevere today. We can endure difficult days when we know that ultimate rest is coming. A focus on the ultimate future sustains us today with vivid hope.

Understanding the ultimate rhythm can help us to release false expectations. In this case, we can—and should—release the erroneous expectation that this life will ever be paradise. That expectation will be fulfilled in eternity, but not before. We will have less frustration and more peace when we accept this reality about today.

So, seize opportunities to do that which will last forever. You will reduce your burnout and increase your fulfillment. When you are engaged in what really matters in heaven, in what is truly significant in God's eyes, you will experience genuine fulfillment and true satisfaction.

Then, embrace the blessing of knowing that what you do matters to God forever. People matter forever. Because of your actions, another person can be touched for eternity. There is a deep sense of fulfillment that comes from knowing that what you are doing pleases God.

Finally, anticipate eternity. That is the source of true and rich hope. In this life full of despair, suffering, and disappointment, hope can be an anchor for your soul. In the darkest days and deepest valleys, the sure prospect of eternity gives sustaining power.

# CONCLUSION
# Living in Rhythm

*Everything has rhythm; everything dances.*

MAYA ANGELOU

When I had my "eureka moment" in New Zealand, I had no idea how rich and deep the concept of rhythm would prove to be, nor how beneficial it would be for my life. Living rhythmically has enabled me to achieve significant freedom from burnout, busyness, and guilt. I've learned that I can accomplish more of what matters with less stress and frustration.

Though I have not unraveled all the implications of living my life in rhythm, my life is so much better today than it was even a few years ago. Gone is the vague floating guilt that I am not living a balanced life. In fact, I have rejected the pursuit of a so-called balanced life. That is no longer my aim. Now I'm asking myself whether my life is in a good rhythm.

Life can still be crazy. As a type A person to the max, I still try to spin too many plates, and I get intense when it's not necessary. In those times, I still need to look at the situation through a rhythm paradigm and apply the appropriate rhythm strategies to bring solutions. However, these days I experience less busyness because I am riding kairos waves as they come. Although the difficulties and challenges are not magically erased, my stress has decreased while my fulfillment and peace have increased as I live rhythmically in each of the five chronos cycles. In short, I have a better life. And I'm confident that you can too.

## What Ever Happened to Mike and Julia Jones?

Mike gave up the insane pursuit of a balanced life. Instead, he has adopted a rhythm approach. As Mike applied the three kairos rhythm strategies and three chronos rhythm strategies, his life improved. He still has a full life, but he is far from burnout.

### RELEASE EXPECTATIONS

Mike released the false expectation that he had to achieve the perfect life in every area right now. Since it was soccer season for his daughter, he quit his basketball league, which meant he put up with some harassment from his friends. Realizing his stage of life—raising young children (who matter for eternity)—Mike released the expectation of competing for "best yard" and the expectation of giving his parents as much time as he had been giving. He also resigned from the community food-pantry board and has slowed down the pace of his MBA program.

### SEIZE OPPORTUNITIES

Mike decided to seize the opportunity to build into the life of his son, Ben, on the Boy Scout campout, letting his parents know he was not coming to see them that weekend, and why. Even though he heard the disappointment in their voices, they affirmed his decision, because after all, Ben is their grandson. Mike and Ben had a blast. Out in the canoes on Sunday morning, Ben asked Mike, "What happens when you die?"

Through Mike's mind ran the haunting question, *What if I had not been here to answer my son?* He was happy to talk about what really matters and enjoy the lake with his son in a canoe. In the weeks that followed, Ben and Mike told stories from the campout over and over again. They posted pictures on their Facebook pages and laughed until they cried as they told the stories to the grandparents over dinner.

### ANTICIPATE WHAT'S NEXT

Next summer, Ben will be just old enough to go to a weeklong wilderness camp in the mountains. Mike has already put in a request to take the week off. He and Ben are dreaming about what they will experience. Together, they are jogging to get in shape for the hikes. The anticipation is helping them both when work and school put on the pressure. In a few months, they will be at camp.

### PACE YOURSELF

Mike and Julia sat down to look at their chronos cycles and make some changes to improve their lives individually, as a couple, and as a family. After reaffirming what really matters to them—their life mission together—they each made lists of regular activities and then began to establish an appropriate frequency for each one. Yard work moved from daily to weekly, which means the yard does not look as good as it once did, but Mike and Julia have more time with Emma and Ben.

### BUILD RITUALS

With work and all the kids' activities, Julia expressed her concern about their unity as a family. She determined, with Mike's support, to build rituals of renewal. Because she had recently read about the importance of breakfast for physical health, they decided to build in a morning ritual with all four family members. They will make, eat, and clean up their breakfast together. While they are eating, each day a different person will read a verse of Scripture and say a prayer for the day. For the health of their marriage, Mike suggested a monthly date night, aiming for the last Friday of each month. They brainstormed the kinds of dates they would enjoy together.

### OSCILLATE BETWEEN WORK AND REST

The conversation about pace and ritual easily led Mike and Julia into talking about the strategy of oscillating between work and rest. Both of them knew they had been terrible at this. Their high stress was due largely to trying to keep a constant pace, which did not allow for occasional seasons of long hours at the job or for times of renewal and recovery.

After the Saturday phone call from his boss, Mike and his work team entered a difficult season. The system breakdown was not a minor problem—it would require weeks of unanticipated work. Knowing that, Mike communicated in advance with his boss, his team, Julia, and the kids. He let them know that, for a five-week stretch, there would be long hours at the office and travel to the client's site. He also announced that when the project was over, everyone on the team would get a four-day weekend. Mike timed the weekend to fall when his kids had a day off from school. He and Julia asked to borrow his parents' RV to take Emma and Ben to their favorite state park.

His parents not only agreed but offered to come along and help watch Emma and Ben.

After some of these strategies were in place, new tensions arose a few months later. Mike and Julia looked again at each natural cycle to see how they could restore a good pace, build life-enhancing rituals, and oscillate between expending energy with replenishing energy. Though their life is still challenging, for the most part it is better, more peaceful, and more fulfilling.

## Your Turn: Taking Action

The richness and depth of the rhythm paradigm has yet to be fully tapped. I hope you will explore further implications and benefits of a rhythm paradigm for your life.[1]

My desire is to help you reduce your stress, burnout, and guilt while gaining more peace, fulfillment, joy, and hope. That can happen as you ride the kairos waves, gliding onto the beach with the wind at your back, and as you follow the chronos cycles, living in sync with the rhythms of life.

### YOUR LIFE

Now it's your turn. If you are still trying to balance your life, let go. Drop the false pursuit of that impossible and foolish goal. What problem has consistently reared its ugly head in your life? Where are you stressed? In your marriage? At work? Your current circumstances? Turn to appendix B, where I have given you blank worksheets. Work through the Rhythm Solution Process. Grab a friend or someone close to you and ask them to help you work through the process.

### YOUR FRIEND

Maybe you are that friend to someone else. Who in your circle is stressed out? Who is caught up in the vain pursuit of balance? Think of someone who could benefit from this book. Share it with them. Help them work through the Rhythm Solution Process to discover a better life.

### YOUR TEAM

If you lead a group of people, imagine the impact of the rhythm paradigm in their lives. Schedule a time with your group to work through the book together, using the questions at the back. Buy the book for your team. How would your team respond to a presentation on the new rhythm paradigm?

### YOUR INFLUENCE

Perhaps you are in a position of more influence. If you are a business leader or a human resources professional, consider how a rhythm paradigm could improve your business. How might you improve morale and productivity on your staff? What if your team was energized to do what it takes to meet a proposal deadline? What if your sales team lived healthier lives? How might a rhythm analysis affect how you look at your business cycles and thus the deployment of your employees in various departments?

What if your business took rhythms seriously? Rather than having employees work forty-hour weeks, week after week, why not envision sixty-five hours one week and fifteen hours the next? I suspect more work would get done over a year in a rhythmic approach with varying hours than in the approach of working a uniform number of hours every week. Some businesses should take a risk and try it.

When it's crunch time, it's appropriate to work long and hard, sometimes all night or all weekend; then it's time to kick back and relax, time to rest and renew. This happens informally in high-trust environments between managers and workers. But could there be a more systemic, rhythmic way of arranging work that harmonizes better with the way life really functions?

### LIFE COACHES

I challenge life coaches to build on the rhythm paradigm to help their clients handle life in a healthier way. Drop the idea of balance and begin working with rhythm as a root concept for envisioning a well-lived life. Develop practical life-management tools based on the concepts of living life in rhythm.

What if business and lifestyle writers begin to change the global conversation from work/life balance to rhythm? What creative ideas might emerge from shifting the paradigm?

How could you envision your life in a new way?
What if you were energized on Monday morning?
What if your family was happy on vacations?
What if your team was fully engaged?
What if you accomplished more with less stress?
What if you truly lived full-out without burnout?

The ancient Greeks said, "Know the time," implying, "Live it well." "Know the critical situation in your life, know that it demands a decision, and what decision, train yourself to recognize as such the decisive point in your life, and to act accordingly."[2] A well-lived life moves in time with the music, of which our lives are but a measure and a part.

No longer will we ask, "Is my life in balance?" The balance myth is busted. "Am I living in a good rhythm?" That is the new question for our lives.

May you experience a great life in rhythm!

# APPENDIX A: Scheduling Your Life Events in Chronos Cycles

Most people have trouble thinking of their lives in terms of the five chronos cycles unless they write something down. To help you organize your thoughts as you begin to make the shift from balance to rhythm, I've included some fill-in charts on the next several pages.

For each of the five chronos cycles, list activities in your life that are common to that cycle. As you fill in the information, be sure to think of examples in all your life roles or stewardships—parent, student, employer, employee, manager, friend, volunteer, church member, citizen, neighbor. Most people find it helpful to zero in on one life role in terms of how they can live that role well in each cycle. You don't have to look at each cycle for every role. Focus on the ones that are most central to your life. For one cycle, you might want to consider your business role, and in another, look through the lens of your family role. The point is to begin to see your roles and responsibilities (your stewardships) from a rhythmic perspective. For each cycle, list your pace (a recurring activity), rituals (a life-enhancing habit or tradition), and oscillations (a deliberate time of either intense exertion or personal renewal).

Don't become overwhelmed. This exercise is intended to set you free, not put you in bondage. Each chart is designed to stimulate your thinking about the activities of your life that fit that cycle. I encourage you to pick one cycle and try one exercise to see if it helps you improve your life. Later, once you've seen how this tool works to improve your life, you can do more.

# My Personal Annual Flow

On the chart below, create an annual cycle for your life. For each month, record activities and events that affect the flow of your life. See pages 230–231 for examples of annual rhythms.

| Month | Annual Rhythms |
|---|---|
| JANUARY | |
| FEBRUARY | |
| MARCH | |
| APRIL | |
| MAY | |
| JUNE | |
| JULY | |
| AUGUST | |
| SEPTEMBER | |
| OCTOBER | |
| NOVEMBER | |
| DECEMBER | |

## Annual Rhythms

Cycles typically have a flow, a recurring pattern. Understanding the flow of a year is particularly powerful because many of us have a hard time seeing a whole year at one time. Think through the cycle of the year. When does it start and end? When are the busy and the slow times? What activities or events demand your time?

### EXAMPLES OF ANNUAL RHYTHMS

**Holidays:** New Year's Day, Valentine's Day, Mother's Day, Memorial Day, Father's Day, Independence Day, Labor Day, Halloween, Veterans Day, Thanksgiving, Christmas, Boxing Day

**Family:** birthdays, wedding anniversaries, vacations, camping, summer camps, reunions, graduations, anniversaries of deaths or tragedies

**Home:** spring-cleaning, planting the garden, sealing the driveway, harvesting the garden, fall cleanup

**School:** first day, open house, Christmas break, spring break, graduation, summer vacation, buying school supplies and clothes, preseason workouts for sports/band/drill team/cheerleading

**Religious:** Lent, Palm Sunday, Easter, Pentecost, Advent, Christmas, Rosh Hashanah, Yom Kippur, Hanukkah, Passover, Ramadan, mission trips, pilgrimages

**Government:** taxes, registrations, renewing licenses, inspections

**Cultural/Societal:** Martin Luther King Jr. Day, May Day, Cinco de Mayo, D-Day, Juneteenth, Pearl Harbor Day

**Work:** company picnic, conferences, trade shows, planning/budgeting, employee reviews, training, fiscal year end, seasonal sales spikes or slumps, Administrative Assistant Day, Boss's Day

**Sports:** training camp, off-season conditioning, special camps, opening day, draft day, play-offs, championship, all-star game, qualifying events

**Seasonal sports:** football, basketball, baseball, soccer, track, volleyball, wrestling, hockey, snow skiing, water skiing, triathlons, marathons, Kentucky Derby, Indy 500, Daytona 500, Ironman Hawaii, Super Bowl, World Series, March Madness, Final Four, Stanley Cup, World Cup

**Health:** physical exam, dental cleaning, eye exam, mammogram, age-related tests; allergies, arthritis, seasonal affective disorder

**Hobbies:** shows, competitions, conventions

**Food:** picnics, cookouts, traditional holiday foods, seasonal fruits and vegetables

**Entertainment:** Academy Awards, Oscars, Grammys, summer blockbusters, holiday movies, favorite TV shows

# My Personal Yearly Cycle

What **yearly** rhythms, rituals, or oscillations would you like to build into your life? On the chart below, draft a few ideas for your yearly cycle. To start, identify a yearly rhythm for one life role. See pages 230–231 for examples of annual rhythms.

| Life Roles | Yearly Pace, Rituals, and Oscillations |
|---|---|
| | |
| | |
| | |
| | |
| | |

# My Personal Quarterly Cycle

What **quarterly** rhythms, rituals, or oscillations would you like to build into your life? On the chart below, draft a few ideas for your quarterly cycle. To start, identify a quarterly rhythm for one life role. See page 237 for examples of quarterly rhythms.

| Life Roles | Quarterly Pace, Rituals, and Oscillations |
|---|---|
| | |
| | |
| | |
| | |
| | |

# My Personal Monthly Cycle

What **monthly** rhythms, rituals, or oscillations would you like to build into your life? On the chart below, draft a few ideas for your monthly cycle. To start, identify a monthly rhythm for one life role. See page 237 for examples of monthly rhythms.

| Life Roles | Monthly Pace, Rituals, and Oscillations |
|---|---|
| | |
| | |
| | |
| | |
| | |

# My Personal Weekly Cycle

What **weekly** rhythms, rituals, or oscillations would you like to build into your life? On the chart below, draft a few ideas for your weekly cycle. To start, identify a weekly rhythm for one life role. See page 238 for examples of weekly rhythms.

| Life Roles | Weekly Pace, Rituals, and Oscillations |
|---|---|
| | |
| | |
| | |
| | |
| | |

# My Personal Daily Cycle

What **daily** rhythms, rituals, or oscillations would you like to build into your life? On the chart below, draft a few ideas for your daily cycle. To start, identify a daily rhythm for one life role. See page 238 for examples of daily rhythms.

| Life Roles | Daily Pace, Rituals, and Oscillations |
| --- | --- |
| | |
| | |
| | |
| | |
| | |

### EXAMPLES OF QUARTERLY RHYTHMS

Oil changes, stock reports, estimated taxes for the self-employed, corporate reports for publicly held companies, assessments of a business plan, goal setting for the next quarter of sales, board meetings, large project at home, planning or reviewing plans, weekend getaway, short Bible study, reading a book, dusting baseboards, cleaning blinds and windows, planning next season's wardrobe, attending big athletic events

### EXAMPLES OF MONTHLY RHYTHMS

Replace furnace or air-conditioning filters, pay bills, do a cleaning projects, buy a gift for a spouse or significant other, go on a big date with your spouse, prepare for school tests and projects, volunteer for something, distribute food to the needy, plan extended time with God, balance bank accounts, review budget, write a letter, have a haircut, color hair, visit friends or family, set goals, close out the month financially, do business reports, challenge for a position on the tennis or racquetball ladder above you, allow for menstruation and energy cycles and mood swings, have a manicure, bathe the dog, read a book, figure out how to repair something that is broken or how to work a new device, prepare your food budget, see a movie, go out to dinner, have a friend or neighbor over for a meal, plan a game night, go to a competition or an event, attend a flea market or antique show or a seminar or a show

### EXAMPLES OF WEEKLY RHYTHMS

Work, weekend activities, TV shows, football games or other sporting events, church or religious services, payday, meetings, yard work, homework, Mondays (starting the week), Fridays (finishing the week), grocery shopping, car maintenance, phone calls to parents or kids away at school, card game, bunco night, meditation, prayer meetings, choir practice, exercise routine, bike ride, youth group meetings, chores (trash day, vacuuming, laundry, cleaning bathrooms, dusting), fishing, movie night, family night, day off, enter data in financial software, classes, piano lessons, ballet lessons, practices, graduate courses, part-time work, business cycles

### EXAMPLES OF DAILY RHYTHMS

Sleeping and waking, eating, making lunches for kids, cooking dinner, commuting to and from work, riding the bus, taking part in after-school activities, brushing teeth, bathing, dressing, exercising, stretching, walking, reading, watching the news, driving kids to school and activities, listening to music, taking coffee breaks, responding to e-mail, networking socially, napping, nursing, playing, relaxing, taking care of daily business cycles (lunchtime rush, walk-in traffic, morning meetings), mailing, reading the newspaper, doing the crossword puzzle or Jumble or Sudoku

# My Personal 21-Segment Week

Envision your week in twenty-one segments, based on the rhythms of a three-part day (morning, afternoon, evening) and a seven-day week. What is your primary focus in each time block? Personal? Family? Work? Volunteer? Fitness? This chart helps you visualize a week at a glance and shows you the rhythm of how you invest your time.

| Day of the Week | Daily Segment | | |
|---|---|---|---|
| | MORNING | AFTERNOON | EVENING |
| MONDAY | | | |
| TUESDAY | | | |
| WEDNESDAY | | | |
| THURSDAY | | | |
| FRIDAY | | | |
| SATURDAY | | | |
| SUNDAY | | | |

## Putting It All Together

Now that you have considered each chronos cycle in detail, take a step back and look at all five cycles together. Each cycle encompasses the ones that are shorter, so they work together at different frequencies.

Looking at all five chronos cycles in one chart can be intimidating, but it can also reduce stress in your life. For one thing, you'll realize you cannot do it all at one time. Different activities of life have their own appropriate frequencies.

How are all these charts going to help you? They help by bringing a lot of diverse information together in one place, which makes it easier to see how you can adapt and adjust your rhythms so they work in harmony with one another. If the charts overwhelm you, it isn't necessary to use them. They're simply a tool to make what is natural more obvious. I hope you find them helpful.

## Your Turn

Using the work you've done on the cycle charts, fill out the following grid for your life. You may not have something for every block, but the exercise will give you an overview that can help you see your whole life at a glance. An at-a-glance perspective may help you see more expectations to release and more opportunities to seize. See page 242 for an example of a completed Life Roles and Chronos Cycles chart.

# Life Roles and Chronos Cycles

| Life Roles | Chronos Cycles | | | | |
|---|---|---|---|---|---|
| | YEARLY | QUARTERLY | MONTHLY | WEEKLY | DAILY |
| MYSELF | | | | | |
| SPOUSE | | | | | |
| PARENT | | | | | |
| EMPLOYEE | | | | | |
| HOBBIES & RECREATION | | | | | |

# Life Roles and Chronos Cycles

| Life Roles | Chronos Cycles | | | | |
|---|---|---|---|---|---|
| | YEARLY | QUARTERLY | MONTHLY | WEEKLY | DAILY |
| MYSELF | *Personal spiritual retreat, seminar, or conference* | *Spend three hours with God; plan next quarter* | *Review last month; plan next month* | *Hour with God; review last week, plan next* | *15 min. to read Bible, pray, and plan the day* |
| SPOUSE | *Vacation* | *Overnight getaway* | *Go out to dinner* | *Alone time at home one night* | *Coffee in the morning* |
| PARENT | *Visit family out of town* | *Weekend outing as a family* | *Personal time with each child* | *Family night* | *Eat dinner together* |
| EMPLOYEE | *Personnel reviews; annual convention* | *Take part in a training event to improve skills* | *Meet personally with each person on my team* | *Fill out weekly report* | *Arrive on time and leave on time* |
| HOBBIES & RECREATION | *Finish major project; enter regional competition* | *Attend an event* | *Do a small project in yard or home* | *Work out at gym three times* | *Read blog from industry expert* |

# APPENDIX B: Rhythm Solution Process Worksheets

To help you apply the six rhythm strategies to your life, I suggest you work through a Rhythm Solution Process using the worksheets on the next pages.

Start by identifying a problem you're facing—at home, work, school, or wherever—and write a brief description.

Next, identify your personal seasons and life stage. These provide the context for applying the six rhythm strategies.

Evaluate the kairos and chronos rhythm strategies to see which one (or ones) will offer the most help for your particular problem. Usually, one to three strategies will directly address a given problem. It may be possible to apply all six strategies to your situation, but that is usually overkill. Most people can take only one or two action steps at any given time, so even if you find a solution that involves multiple steps, I strongly suggest you start with just one or two of the most powerful steps and then move to the next ones as needed.

To apply the three kairos rhythm strategies, answer the following questions: What expectations can I release to achieve peace amid my circumstances? What opportunities can I seize to find fulfillment in my current situation? In what ways can I begin to anticipate what's next, in order to build hope?

To apply the three chronos rhythm strategies, answer the following questions: How can I pace myself to achieve optimum frequency and flow? How can I build rituals (traditions and habits) that will enhance my life? How can I oscillate between work and rest to take full advantage of both?

If you need more worksheets, they are available to download for free at www.yourlifeinrhythm.com.

# Rhythm Solution Process Worksheet

YOUR NAME: ______________________________

| | |
|---|---|
| Identify the Problem | |
| Identify Personal Seasons and Life Stages | PERSONAL SEASONS:<br><br>LIFE STAGE: |
| Apply Kairos Rhythm Strategies | RELEASE EXPECTATIONS: |
| | SEIZE OPPORTUNITIES: |
| | ANTICIPATE WHAT'S NEXT: |
| Apply Chronos Rhythm Strategies | SET YOUR PACE (FREQUENCY AND FLOW): |
| | BUILD RITUALS (TRADITIONS AND HABITS): |
| | OSCILLATE BETWEEN WORK AND REST: |

# Rhythm Solution Process Worksheet

YOUR NAME: ______________________________

| | |
|---|---|
| Identify the Problem | |
| Identify Personal Seasons and Life Stages | PERSONAL SEASONS:<br><br>LIFE STAGE: |
| Apply Kairos Rhythm Strategies | RELEASE EXPECTATIONS: |
| | SEIZE OPPORTUNITIES: |
| | ANTICIPATE WHAT'S NEXT: |
| Apply Chronos Rhythm Strategies | SET YOUR PACE (FREQUENCY AND FLOW): |
| | BUILD RITUALS (TRADITIONS AND HABITS): |
| | OSCILLATE BETWEEN WORK AND REST: |

# Questions for Group Discussion and Personal Reflection

## Introduction

1. Why are you interested in reading this book?
2. What questions do you have about the book?
3. What issues do you hope the book will address?
4. What objections or concerns do you have even before you've read it?
5. What do you hope you will get out of it?

## Part I: Rhythm

1. Why do you think balance is such a popular idea?
2. What problems do you see with the concept of balance?
3. What makes rhythm such a powerful alternative to balance?
4. What about rhythm is attractive to you?
5. What are the differences between the two kinds of rhythm: *chronos* and *kairos*? Give some examples.
6. What have you gained from the book thus far?

## Part II: Kairos Rhythm Strategies

1. What are the two main kinds of kairos rhythms?
2. Why might it be valuable to identify your personal seasons and current life stage?
3. What personal seasons are you in right now?
4. What's your present life stage? Are you just entering it, in the middle of it, or coming to the end of it?
5. How will the next stage on the horizon be different from the stage you are in now?
6. What false expectations have you been living with that you could release to find more peace?
7. What opportunities could you seize in this time of your life?
8. What do you anticipate will come next in your life that gives you hope today?
9. Of the three kairos rhythm strategies, which is most powerful for you? Why?

## Part III: Chronos Rhythm Strategies

1. What are the five chronos cycles? Why are they important to a good life?
2. What activities in your life could you put on a better frequency in the five cycles?
3. In which cycle do want to develop a more healthy flow?
4. What rituals could you establish in your business or personal world that would enhance your life?
5. How could you better oscillate between work and rest in one of the five cycles?

## Part IV: A Rhythm Solution Process

1. What is an issue or situation in your life to which you would like to apply the six rhythm strategies?
2. How did or could the Rhythm Solution Process help you?

## Part V: Ultimate Rhythm and Conclusion

1. What is your understanding of eternity? Are you prepared to meet God one day?
2. How can seeing from an eternal perspective help you live a better life today?
3. What is the most important or most helpful idea you have gained from this book?
4. How will you improve your life with what you have learned?
5. What could you do to extend or expand the ideas in this book?
6. How do you think your friends will respond to the principles of rhythm?

# Notes


**Introduction: The Burden of "Balance"**

1. Stephen R. Covey, "Work-Life Balance: A Different Cut," *Forbes*, March 21, 2007, http://www.forbes.com/careers/2007/03/19/covey-work-life-lead-careers-worklife07-cz_sc_0319covey.html.
2. Jim Bird, "Work-Life Balance: Doing It Right and Avoiding the Pitfalls," WorkLifeBalance.com, 2006, http://www.worklifebalance.com/assets/pdfs/article3.pdf.

**Chapter 1: How I Got Rhythm**

1. "What Is Fitness?" *The CrossFit Journal*, October 2002, 4, http://library.crossfit.com/free/pdf/CFJ-trial.pdf.
2. Jim Loehr and Tony Schwartz, *The Power of Full Engagement* (New York: Free Press, 2003), 30.
3. Ibid., 29.
4. Ibid., 30.

**Chapter 2: Our Busy Lives and the Burden of Balance**

1. Stephen R. Covey, A. Roger Merrill, and Rebecca R. Merrill, *First Things First: To Live, to Love, to Learn, to Leave a Legacy* (New York: Simon & Schuster, Fireside, 1994), 119.

**Chapter 4: Kairos and Chronos Rhythms**

1. Over the centuries, the words' fields of meaning shifted slightly. In ancient Greece, *chronos* and *kairos* were more distinct; later, they tended to overlap as nearly synonymous, such as in the New Testament.
2. *Exegetical Dictionary of the New Testament*, Horst Balz and Gerhard Schneider, eds. (Grand Rapids: Eerdmans, 1990–1993), 3:488–489.
3. *Theological Dictionary of the New Testament*, electronic edition, Gerhard Kittel and Gerhard Friedrich, eds., Geoffrey Bromiley, trans. (Grand Rapids: Eerdmans, 1964–1976), 9:593.
4. Ibid., 3:455–464.
5. See 2 Timothy 4:6; Luke 1:20.

**Chapter 5: Your Personal Seasons and Life Stages**

1. Choon-Leong Seow, "Ecclesiastes," in *The Anchor Bible Commentary* (New York: Doubleday, 1997), 171.

2. The Hebrew word *yapeh* in Ecclesiastes 3:11 means "right, proper, appropriate, good." It is not an aesthetic judgment, as the common translation "beautiful" might suggest. See Seow, "Ecclesiastes," 162. See also Tremper Longman, *The Book of Ecclesiastes* (Grand Rapids: Eerdmans, 1998), 112.
3. Roy Zuck, *Reflecting with Solomon: Selected Studies on the Book of Ecclesiastes* (Grand Rapids: Baker, 1994), 217, 222. See especially quote by George R. Castellino.
4. Ibid., 259, 264.
5. Elisabeth Kübler-Ross, *On Death and Dying* (New York: Macmillan, 1969). See also Elisabeth Kübler-Ross and David Kessler, *On Grief and Grieving: Finding the Meaning of Grief Through the Five Stages of Loss* (New York: Scribner, 2005).
6. http://changingminds.org/disciplines/change_management/kubler_ross/kubler_ross.htm (accessed on April 28, 2007).
7. William Shakespeare, *As You Like It*, 2.7.138–142. See the entire soliloquy for Shakespeare's take on life stages.
8. In *Passages*, Gail Sheehy summarizes Erikson's point: "In the first adult stage, the key issue is intimacy, and the alternative isolation. His next criterion for continued growth is generativity, the process by which the individual becomes paternal and creative in a new sense, feeling a voluntary commitment to guide new generations and younger associates. The final stage presents the opportunity for integrity and might be said to represent the point at which the midlife crisis has been successfully resolved" ([New York: Dutton, 1976], 18–19).
9. Sheehy, *Passages*, xi.
10. Gail Sheehy, *New Passages* (New York: Ballantine, 1995), 11. Also, see pages 36–44 and 424–425 for brief descriptions of life stages at each decade.
11. Ibid., 3–4.
12. Sheehy, *Passages*, 27.
13. Kenneth H. Cooper and Tyler C. Cooper, with William Proctor, *Start Strong, Finish Strong: Prescriptions for a Lifetime of Great Health* (New York: Avery, 2007), 7; italics in the original.
14. Ibid., 8.

**Chapter 6: Release Expectations**

1. William Blake, "Eternity," in *William Blake: The Complete Poems* (New York: Penguin, 1978), 153.

**Chapter 7: Seize Opportunities**

1. *Rev!* magazine, May/June, 2007.

**Chapter 9: The Five Chronos Cycles**

1. Stephen R. Covey, A. Roger Merrill, and Rebecca R. Merrill, *First Things First: To Live, to Love, to Learn, to Leave a Legacy* (New York: Simon & Schuster, Fireside, 1994), 16.
2. In contrast, the lengths of a second, minute, and hour *are* culturally invented, artificial, fractional divisions of a day.
3. "Since our Time is reduced to a Standard, and the Bullion of the Day minted out into Hours, the Industrious know how to employ every Piece of Time to a real Advantage in their different Professions: And he that is prodigal of his Hours, is, in effect, a Squanderer of Money. I remember a notable Woman, who was fully sensible of the intrinsic Value of *Time*. Her Husband was a Shoemaker, and an excellent Craftsman, but never minded how the Minutes passed. In vain did she inculcate to him, *That Time is Money*. He had too much Wit to apprehend her, and it prov'd his Ruin. When at the Alehouse among his idle Companions, if one remark'd that the Clock struck Eleven. *What is that*, says he, *among us all?* If she sent him Word by the Boy, that it had struck Twelve; *Tell her to be easy, it can never be more*. If, that it had struck One, *Bid her be comforted, for it can never be less*" (Benjamin Franklin, *Poor Richard's Almanac*, 1751).
4. See Franz Halberg, *Introduction to Chronobiology*, Halberg Chronobiology Center, University of Minnesota, 1994, http://www.msi.umn.edu/~halberg/introd/index.html.
5. Russell G. Foster and Leon Kreitzman, *Rhythms of Life: The Biological Clocks that Control the Daily Lives of Every Living Thing* (New Haven, CT: Yale, 2004), 3.
6. Ibid., 4. Chronobiology is no longer a minor science. "It is now being studied in major universities and medical centers around the world," note Susan Perry and Jim Dawson in *The Secrets Our Body Clocks Reveal* (Rawson Associates, 1988). "There are chronobiologists working for the National Aeronautics and Space Administration (NASA), as well as for the National Institutes of Health and other government laboratories. Chronobiology is becoming part of the mainstream of science, and it is changing our way of looking at life and time."
7. Ibid., 5.
8. See works on the anthropic principle, such as Guillermo Gonzalez and Jay W. Richards, *The Privileged Planet* (Regnery, 2004), for more information on the fragile and special features of our planet that allow life to flourish.
9. The two moments when the inclination of Earth's rotation axis has maximum effect are the solstices. An equinox is the event when the sun

can be observed to be directly above the equator; on these dates, night and day are nearly the same length.
10. Daniel J. Boorstin, *The Discoverers* (New York: Random House, 1983), 4.
11. Pitirim A. Sorokin, *Sociocultural Causality, Space, Time* (Durham, NC: Duke University, 1943), quoted in "Social Rhythms, Cycles, and Clocks," http://www.trinity.edu/~mkearl/time-3.html.
12. "Weeks" have varied in length from three to nineteen days in past cultures. In parts of Africa along the Congo River, short weeks are found. The Mayas of the Yucatán had clusters of five-day weeks. Emperor Constantine established the seven-day week of the Roman calendar in AD 321; he also set Sunday as the first day of the week. However, its historical origin before Rome is difficult to precisely discern. It is an ancient practice of very early origin.
13. Eviatar Zerubavel, *The Seven Day Circle* (Chicago: University of Chicago, 1985), 9.
14. Perry and Dawson, *Secrets Our Body Clocks Reveal*, 20–21.
15. Jeremy Campbell, *Winston Churchill's Afternoon Nap* (New York: Simon & Schuster, 1986), 79. Campbell also writes: "These circaseptan, or about weekly, rhythms are one of the major surprises turned up by modern chronobiology. Fifteen years ago, few scientists would have expected that seven-day biological cycles would prove to be so widespread and so long established in the living world. They are of very ancient origin, appearing in primitive one-celled organisms, and are thought to be present even in bacteria, the simplest form of life now existing." In an article titled "God's Mysterious Seven Day Cycle in Plants, Animals, and Man!" Ken Westby writes, "One of Franz Halberg's amazing discoveries is that of an innate rhythm—about seven days—occurring in a giant alga some five million years old on the evolutionary time line. Because this microscopic cell resembles a graceful champagne glass, the alga (plant) is popularly known as mermaid's wineglass (*Acetabularia mediterranea*). When this 'primitive' alga is subjected to artificial schedules of alternating light and dark spans of varying length over many days, this single intact cell is somehow able to translate all that manipulation of light and darkness into the measurement of a seven-day week! . . . If the seven-day week is an invention of culture and religion, as most historians would have us believe, how do we explain innate circaseptan rhythms in 'primitive' algae, rats, plants and face flies?" http://www.biblestudy.org/godsrest/mysterious-seven-day-cycle-in-plants-animals-man-1.html.

**Chapter 11: Build Life-Enhancing Rituals**

1. "Ritual," Dictionary.com, *Dictionary.com Unabridged (v 1.1)*, Random House, Inc., http://dictionary.reference.com/browse/ritual.

2. William Doherty, "Intentional Marriage: Your Rituals Will Set You Free" (banquet keynote address, Smart Marriages Conference, Denver, CO, 2007), http://www.smartmarriages.com/intentionalmarriage.html.
3. Jim Loehr and Tony Schwartz, *The Power of Full Engagement* (New York: Free Press, 2003), 166.
4. Friesen writes: "Various studies have examined the neurobiological impact of participation in rituals [d'Aquili, et al., (1979)]. These investigations show that rituals produce positive limbic discharges which lead to warmth and closeness among people. Rituals tend to stimulate both left and right parts of the brain so that the 'two hemispheres of the brain spill over into each other.' The result may be deep emotional experiences, such as a 'shiver down the back.' These experiences have the effect of facilitating personal integration and the feeling of well-being. Rituals tend to combine both digital and analogic levels of information so that logical and verbal methods of communication are combined with nonverbal symbolic methods. Rituals thus hold a level of meaning and significance that words alone cannot capture" (John D. Friesen, "Rituals and Family Strength," *Direction Journal* 19, no. 1 [Spring 1990]: 39–48), http://www.directionjournal.org/article/?654.
5. Peggy Patten, "The Role of Ritual in Strengthening Family Ties: An Interview with William Doherty," Burlington Little School, http://www.nvo.com/bls/articlesandnewsletters/article.nhtml?uid=10004 (accessed November 3, 2008; site now discontinued).
6. Family Rituals—Research on Family Rituals, http://family.jrank.org/pages/574/Family-Rituals-Research-on-Family-Rituals.html.
7. Barbara H. Fiese and others, "A Review of 50 Years of Research on Naturally Occurring Family Routines and Rituals: Cause for Celebration?" *Journal of Family Psychology*, Syracuse University 16, no. 4.
8. Adapted from Carol J. Plate, "Family Holiday Traditions," http://unlforfamilies.unl.edu/Time/Family/TimeFamilyHolidayTraditions.htm.
9. Doherty, "Intentional Marriage."
10. See, for example, "Who We Are/What the New Monasticism Is," New Monasticism, http://www.newmonasticism.org. Also, Christine Sine refers to monastic practices in her excellent book, *Sacred Rhythms: Finding a Peaceful Pace in a Hectic World* (Baker, 2003).
11. See more in Loehr and Schwartz, *Power of Full Engagement*, 14.

**Chapter 12: Oscillate Between Work and Rest**

1. Eugene H. Peterson, *The Message: The Bible in Contemporary Language* (Colorado Springs: NavPress, 2002).
2. "The biblical pattern of eating swung between the fast and the feast.

Fasting, the abstinence of food, was a sign of repentance and utter dependence on God. Feasting, no less a spiritual discipline, was a sign of the goodness of God. Though most of the Israelites' meals were no doubt simple fare, they knew both seasons of abstinence and the festivals of indulgence (the three most significant being Unleavened Bread, Weeks, and Booths)" (Maxie D. Dunnam, Gordon MacDonald, and Donald W. McCullough, *Mastering Personal Growth* [Sisters, OR: Multnomah, 1992], 123).

3. Larry Osborne, in his chapter "Seeking Balance: Does God Give a Rip?" in *A Contrarian's Guide to Knowing God: Spirituality for the Rest of Us* (Multnomah, 2007), lists multiple biblical people who were not well-balanced by today's standards. Craig Groeschel, in his March 24, 2008, blog entry, "The Myth of the Balanced Life," writes, "In my opinion the balanced life is unachievable and unbiblical." Nancy Ortberg, in *Looking for God*, says, "I believe balance is a myth. A unicorn" (Carol Stream, IL: Tyndale, 2008), 69.
4. Jim Loehr and Tony Schwartz, *The Power of Full Engagement* (New York: Free Press, 2003), 13.
5. Ibid., 12.
6. http://www.futurevisions.org/energy_least.htm.
7. Loehr and Schwartz, *Power of Full Engagement*, 200.
8. Ibid.
9. Ibid.
10. Mihaly Csikszentmihalyi, *Flow* (New York: Harper & Row, 1990), 3.
11. Loehr and Schwartz, *Power of Full Engagement*, 28.
12. Ibid., 29.
13. Matthew Kelly, *The Rhythm of Life: Living Every Day with Passion and Purpose* (New York: Simon & Schuster, Fireside, 1999), 294.
14. Loehr and Schwartz, *Power of Full Engagement*, 12.
15. Robert J. Banks, *The Tyranny of Time* (Downers Grove, IL: InterVarsity, 1983), 224.
16. Ibid., 223–224.
17. Arthur Miller, *Death of a Salesman*, Act I, in *The Portable Arthur Miller*, updated edition (New York: Penguin, 1995), 23.
18. Kay Judge and Maxine Barish-Wreden, "Take Two Vacations and Call Me in the Morning," *Dallas Morning News*, July 1, 2008. Article can also be read online at http://www.relax411online.com/?q=node/108.
19. Ibid.
20. Randy Frazee, *Making Room for Life: Trading Chaotic Lifestyles for Connected Relationships* (Grand Rapids: Zondervan, 2003), 60.
21. Leslie Garcia, "How Getting a Good Night's Sleep Helps during the Day," *Dallas Morning News*, July 22, 2008. Story can be read online at

http://www.dallasnews.com/sharedcontent/dws/fea/healthyliving2/stories/DN-nh_sleep_0722liv.ART.State.Edition1.2ca4973.html.

22. National Institute of Mental Health, "'Power Nap' Prevents Burnout; Morning Sleep Perfects a Skill," July 2, 2002, http://www.nimh.nih.gov/science-news/2002/power-nap-prevents-burnout-morning-sleep-perfects-a-skill.shtml.
23. Sara Mednick, Take a Nap, LLC, http://www.saramednick.com.
24. How long is a good nap? See "Ten Benefits of Power Napping and How to Do It," http://ririanproject.com/2007/09/05/10-benefits-of-power-napping-and-how-to-do-it. The Nano-Nap (10–20 seconds): Sleep studies haven't yet concluded whether there are benefits to these brief intervals, like when you nod off on someone's shoulder on the train. The Micro-Nap (2–5 minutes): Shown to be surprisingly effective at shedding sleepiness. The Mini-Nap (5–20 minutes): Increases alertness, stamina, motor learning, and motor performance. The Original Power Nap (20 minutes): Includes the benefits of the micro and the mini, but additionally improves muscle memory and clears the brain of useless built-up information, which helps with long-term memory (remembering facts, events, and names). The Lazy Man's Nap (50–90 minutes): Includes slow-wave plus REM sleep; good for improving perceptual processing; also when the system is flooded with human growth hormone, great for repairing bones and muscles.

**Chapter 13: Putting It All Together**

1. Henry Hazlitt, *Thinking as a Science* (New York: E. P. Dutton, 1916; fifth printing, 1920), 17.

**Chapter 14: Seeing from Eternity**

1. Choon-Leong Seow, "Ecclesiastes" in *The Anchor Bible Commentary* (New York: Doubleday, 1997), 163. There is an academic debate over the meaning of the Hebrew word used for "eternity." See note 14 for Ecclesiastes 3:11 in the NET Bible (http://www.bible.org/netbible/index.htm) for an excellent summary of the arguments for the three main positions.
2. Michael Eaton, "Ecclesiastes" in *Tyndale Old Testament Commentaries* (Downers Grove, IL: InterVarsity, 1983), 81.
3. Augustine, *Confessions*, 1.1, author's paraphrase.
4. Robert J. Banks, *The Tyranny of Time* (Downers Grove, IL: InterVarsity, 1983), 261.

**Conclusion: Living in Rhythm**

1. For instance, biblical scholars could enhance our understanding of time and rhythm by studying the meaning of time in the Old and

New Testaments. Theologians could investigate the theology of time as both linear and cyclical. Psychologists, sociologists, and pastors could explore various kairos seasons and the implications of discoveries from chronobiology. The concept of life stages bears much more research. If we better understand the stages of adult life, we might be less surprised and more prepared for what comes next in our lives.

2. Gerhard Delling, quoted in Gerhard Kittel and Gerhard Friedrich, eds., Geoffrey Bromiley, trans., *Theological Dictionary of the New Testament*, electronic edition (Grand Rapids: Eerdmans, 1964–1976), 3:455–464.

# About the Author

## BRUCE B. MILLER

God has given Bruce the privilege of serving as husband to his wife, Tamara, since 1983 and father to their five children. They are also blessed with their grandchildren. God used Bruce to plant Christ Fellowship in McKinney, Texas where he currently serves as senior pastor (CFhome.org). In his spare time, he loves spending time with Tamara, playing racquetball, using a chainsaw and sitting by an open fire with his chocolate Labrador, Calvin.

His passion for leadership development led to his first book, *The Leadership Baton*, written with Jeff Jones and Rowland Forman. Bruce's heart to see people live more joyful, fulfilled lives sparked the writing of *Your Life in Rhythm*, the forerunner to *Your Church in Rhythm* which applies the concepts of rhythmic living to local churches (BruceBMiller.com).

Bruce developed the innovative six-step WISDOM Process© which serves as a learning engine in the study guides for his books *Big God in a Chaotic World—A Fresh Look at Daniel; When God Makes No Sense—A Fresh Look at Habakkuk; Sexuality—Approaching Controversial Issues with Grace, Truth and Hope, and Same-Sex Marriage—A Bold Call to the Church in Response to the Supreme Court's Decision.*

Bruce graduated Phi Beta Kappa from the University of Texas at Austin with a B.A. in Plan II, the Honors Liberal Arts Program ('82); received a master's degree in Theology from Dallas Theological Seminary ('86); and did doctoral work at the University of Texas at Dallas in the History of Ideas (focus on philosophical hermeneutics, Hans-Georg Gadamer, and post-modernism). He taught theology for four years at Dallas Theological Seminary.

Bruce speaks and consults around the world. He founded the Centers for Church Based Training and served as Chairman of the Board for 12 years (http://ccbt.org). Bruce founded and leads Dadlin ministries, an organization committed to helping people develop wisdom for life.

You can follow Bruce on:

**Twitter** (http://twitter.com/Bruce_B_Miller) or

**Facebook** (https://www.facebook.com/BruceBMillerAuthor)

**Blog** (BruceBMiller.com)

To invite Bruce to speak, contact him at:

**Website** (BruceBMiller.com)

# Other Resources

*The publishing ministry of Dadlin ministries—an organization committed to helping people develop wisdom for life.*

Dadlin Press
*wisdom for life*

Resources by **Bruce B. Miller**:

*The Leadership Baton*
Equips you with a solution to the need for quality leaders in local churches. Miller provides you with a biblical vision, a holistic approach and a comprehensive plan.

*Your Life in Rhythm*
Offers a realistic way to overcome our crazy, overly busy, stressed lives. Exposes the myth of living a "balanced" life. Miller presents "rhythmic living" as a new paradigm for relieving guilt and stress, so we can accomplish more of what matters most in life—with more freedom, peace, fulfillment and hope.

*Your Church in Rhythm*

Most pastors try to do everything at once, and they feel guilty if even one aspect of their church ministry is neglected in the process. Instead, Miller proposes replacing this exhausting notion of "balance" with the true-to-life concept of "rhythm." Churches, just like people, should focus on the seasons and the cycles of ministry programs. That way, leaders can avoid burnout by focusing only on each issue at the time that it matters most.

*Big God in a Chaotic World—A Fresh Look at Daniel*
Shows we can live faithfully in this sinful, out-of-control world when we get a fresh vision of our big God. Daniel opens our eyes to see the God who is bigger than the problems in our world, bigger than all our fears, fires and lions.

*Same-Sex Marriage—A Bold Call to the Church in Response to the Supreme Court's Decision*

In response to this cultural crisis, the church should step up with a Christlike response that stuns the world, and draws people to Jesus Christ with counter-cultural love.

*Sexuality—Approaching Controversial Issues with Grace, Truth and Hope*
Addresses the purposes of sex in marriage, singleness, cohabitation, homosexuality (and more), with fresh biblical insights filled with grace.

**Coming Soon:**
*Same-Sex Wedding—Should I Attend?*
*When God Makes No Sense—A Fresh Look at Habakkuk*
*Never the Same—A Fresh Look at the Sermon on the Mount*
*Miracles—A Fresh Look at Jesus*

For more information on current and upcoming books, go to BruceBMiller.com.

Dadlin Press
*wisdom for life*

McKinney, TX 75070

Made in the USA
Coppell, TX
18 July 2025

52081047R00154